PREGNANCY GUIDE AND ENNEAGRAM

2-in-1 Book

First-Time Mom: What to Expect When You're Expecting + Enneagram: Uncover Your Unique Path with The 9 Personality Types (Guide for Beginners)

FIRST-TIME MOM: PREPARE YOURSELF FOR PREGNANCY

A New Mom's Survival Handbook With All the Helpful Tips & Information You Need While Expecting + 30 Day Meal Plan for Pregnancy

Table of Contents

Introduction 8
Chapter 1 - The Journey Begins 11
    An Essential Quit List for All Pregnant Women 11
    The Truth About Weight Gain During Pregnancy 15
    What About Stretch Marks? 17
    5 Health-Boosting Supplements for Mom and Baby 19
Chapter 2 - The First Trimester 23
    10 Common Symptoms of the First Trimester & How to Manage Them 24
    When to Call Your Doctor 28
    5 Ways Your Body Will Change in the First Trimester 29
    What is a Doula & How Can They Help? 31
Chapter 3 - The Second Trimester 34
    Pelvic Floor Exercises that All Mothers Must Know 34
    5 Ways to Start Bonding With Your Baby 36
    Watch Out For These Signs of Preeclampsia 38
    The Best Ways to Exercise in the Second Trimester 39
    10 Fun Ideas for the Second Trimester 40
Chapter 4 - The Third Trimester 45
    Every First-Time Mom's To-Do List for the Third Trimester 45
    Breastfeeding vs. Formula Feeding 48
    Tackling Third-Trimester Insomnia 50

Labor Signals & What They Mean 52

Braxton Hicks Contractions vs. Labor Contractions 53

How Do You Induce Labor Safely and Naturally? 54

Chapter 5 - Preparing for the Big Day 57

Pack These 13 Essentials in Your Hospital Bag 57

22 New-Baby & First-Time Mom Necessities 60

How to Start Creating a Birth Plan 67

Chapter 6 - Childbirth & Labor 70

10 Less-Known Things You Should Know About Vaginal Childbirth & Labor 70

4 Things to Do for a Safer C-Section 74

The Lowdown on Epidural Anesthesia 74

7 Helpful Tricks for Pushing that Baby Out 76

The Best Positions for Pushing with an Epidural 77

7 Little-Known Things about C-Sections 78

Chapter 7 - Postpartum Care 80

What Every Mother Needs to Do after Giving Birth 80

9 Completely Normal Long-Term & Short-Term Effects of Pregnancy and Childbirth 81

How to Help the Body Heal from Birth 85

Everything You Need to Know About Postpartum Depression ... 87

9 Soul-Soothing Self-Care Ideas for a First-Time Mom 88

Chapter 8 - Your Newborn Baby 92

11 Things You Should Know About Newborn Babies 92

6 Must-Know Rules About Formula-Feeding 94

Foods to Limit or Avoid While Breastfeeding 95

How to Prevent Sudden Infant Death Syndrome 97
It's Bath Time! 100
Conclusion **104**
30 Day Meal Plan **107**
Week 1 107
Week 2 108
Week 3 109
Week 4 110
Week 5 112
Snack List 113

Introduction

You're about to become a mother for the first time – congratulations! These months will be some of the most special in your entire life and also, some of the most challenging. As overjoyed as you are to be bringing a new life into the world, chances are you're also incredibly nervous. Carrying a child is no walk in the park, as you've likely heard. And when it's your first time, it's all new and uncertain territory. You're probably anxious about the ways your body is changing, the new sensations you're experiencing, and above all, you're wondering how on earth you can keep your baby healthy when there is such an overload of information about what to do and not do. If you're feeling overwhelmed by this new chapter in your life, no one would blame you.

Thing is, pregnancy does not have to be a time of confusion and anxiety. This may be an entirely new experience, but that doesn't mean it has to be fraught with worry. All you need is the right guidance and helpful, accurate information that is easily accessible to you at all times. With this book by your side, you can transition confidently into your role as a first-time mom. Each chapter will guide you through the many steps of your pregnancy, so you'll never feel uncertain. No more stress or anxiety. Just total awareness and all the preparation you need to be the most competent mom for your new baby.

In this book, each trimester will be completely demystified. I'll get in-depth about each specific trimester and what your baby needs from you in each one. You'll understand your symptoms, how to manage them, activities to avoid at all costs, what to eat for your baby's optimal health, how to prepare for labor and birth – and so much more. If you have a question, I have an answer. Just take a peek in this book whenever you're not sure about something.

First-Time Mom

As the proud mom of five beautiful and healthy children, it's safe to say I am very experienced when it comes to pregnancy and baby care. I vividly remember what it was like to be pregnant for the first time – I devoured a heap of books, frustrated that I couldn't find *just one book* to cover everything. For over a decade I coached friends through their first pregnancies, began the popular 'Happy Mom, Happy Baby' club in my hometown, and of course, I expanded my knowledge as each of my other babies came along. No two pregnancies are alike – but what I've learned is that the best advice and support always comes from an experienced mom.

With the best advice under your belt, you'll ride the waves of pregnancy with confidence. You can focus on your own physical and emotional well-being so that, when your baby comes, he or she is brought into the best possible environment. No mom will tell you that pregnancy is easy, but what it *can* be is a clarifying and empowering experience for the lifetime of motherhood that is to come. With this book, you'll have all the tools you need to get on the right path.

The people I coach and the friends I've supported through first-time pregnancies continue to thank me to this day. While every mom knows there's no such thing as a pregnancy 'expert,' I've been told I come as close as you can get. The secrets I share with the people I help are exactly what I will be unveiling in this book. You, too, can reap the benefits I've seen other mothers blossom with.

When it comes to your pregnancy preparation, there's no such thing as doing it later. Your budding baby needs specific conditions *now*; you're either preparing or you're not. The early days are some of the most crucial for your baby's development, as you are still at risk of a miscarriage. Make sure you get the right help as soon as possible, so you can get your baby on the path towards optimal health.

The chance to be a good mom doesn't just arise when your baby is born; the chance is here already. It is now. The choices you make while your child is in your belly have the potential to affect his or her entire life. Don't stumble into motherhood. Take strong, empowered steps. As you turn the page, feel assured that the first strong step begins.

Chapter 1 - The Journey Begins

With a decade of pregnancy coaching behind me, I've noticed many similarities between all first-time moms, especially in the early days. Once the thrill and joy from their good news has settled, they have the same concerns. "How much do I have to change my current lifestyle?" is the general gist of most of their questions. They ask me, "How can I stop myself from gaining so much weight?" or "How can I prevent stretch marks?" New moms tend to feel guilty for asking these questions, but there's no reason to! A baby changes everything and that includes your body. It's okay to have moments where you feel overwhelmed – where it feels like the world is shifting under your feet. Be patient with yourself and know that it's a lot easier to navigate when you take it one step at a time.

In this chapter, I'll cover all the first concerns that I've heard from first-time moms. Everything you need to know right off the bat is here, as it'll likely apply to your entire pregnancy. The journey has begun – embrace it!

An Essential Quit List for All Pregnant Women

When you're pregnant, the last thing you should be doing is business as usual. You are no longer the only person affected by your diet and habits; there's a new life on board now. And in some cases, 'business as usual' can have disastrous consequences on the new life you're creating. Once you know you're expecting, you'll need to cull every single habit that's on this quit list. This is non-negotiable. It's absolutely essential that you and your baby are safe and healthy.

1. **Smoking and Second-Hand Smoke**

    Smoking can have an extremely negative impact on your baby's health and your pregnancy as a whole. Pregnant women who smoke are much more likely to have a miscarriage, go through premature labor, or an ectopic pregnancy. And believe it or not, second-hand smoke is just as harmful. Exposure can lead to the same consequences as smoking and may even result in behavioral or learning issues in the growing child.

2. Chores that Involve Strong Chemicals and Fumes

Pregnant women don't get a free pass on all household chores but you should definitely avoid duties that involve heavy chemicals such as oven cleaners, aerosol products, and pesticides. It's difficult to steer clear of all chemicals – so if you're unsure if what you're using is safe, read the warning label and instructions. If you're the sole cleaner of the house, consider turning to natural options like baking soda and vinegar which can often do an equally efficient job. In addition to this, always wear rubber gloves when handling cleaning products and make sure a few windows are open so your home gets excellent ventilation. These practices can make all the difference!

3. All Alcohol

By now, quitting alcohol is well-known as an essential part of a healthy pregnancy – and for good reasons! When a pregnant woman drinks alcohol, it reaches her baby. This is because alcohol can pass through the bloodstream into the placenta. This can damage the baby's brain and organs, resulting in birth defects, brain damage, stillbirth, a miscarriage, and more. All types of alcohol must be avoided during pregnancy, including wine, beer, and liquor.

4. Over 200mg of Caffeine

You don't need to give up coffee or green tea entirely when you're expecting – but you should avoid consuming large amounts. Too much caffeine puts women at a higher risk of miscarriage. On top of this, studies have shown that caffeine can enter the placenta; this means that when you ingest caffeine, so does your baby. Caffeine may just give *you* a light buzz, but think of the effect it can have on a newly formed being without a developed metabolism. If you're a coffee drinker, limit yourself to one cup a day and no more. Keep in mind that many sodas and energy drinks also contain caffeine. If you enjoy drinking these types of beverages, pay close attention to how much caffeine they contain.

5. High-Mercury Fish

Fish can be highly beneficial for a pregnant woman's diet, but high-mercury fish are a whole different deal. Women who are pregnant or nursing are advised to steer clear of fish with high amounts of mercury in their meat. This means no tuna, shark, mackerel, and swordfish.

6. Unpasteurized Dairy Products

Pregnant women *and* infants should steer clear of unpasteurized dairy. In other words, anything made from raw milk such as unpasteurized cheese and obviously, raw milk itself. The pasteurization process kills harmful bacteria – so when you consume raw milk, there's a possibility it could contain dangerous microorganisms with the potential to pose life-threatening consequences to you and your child. A study published by the Minnesota Department of Public Health revealed that one in six people who drink raw milk will get sick. It is advised that all pregnant women play it safe and avoid consuming all forms of raw milk from any animal.

7. Cleaning Cat Litter

If you own a cat, pass the cat litter-cleaning duties to your partner, family

member, or other housemates. As adorable as your cat is, he or she could be a carrier of the *Toxoplasma Gondii* parasite which could be transferred to you through contact with your cat's waste. This parasite can cause an infection called Toxoplasmosis and if you're infected while pregnant, it can result in big problems for the baby or your pregnancy, such as stillbirth or miscarriage. If there's no one else to change the cat litter, then take extra precautions by wearing gloves, only feeding your cat dry food, washing your hands thoroughly afterward and keeping your cat indoors.

8. **Heavy-Lifting**

Pregnant women should avoid all forms of heavy-lifting, as the strain caused can do different types of damage, depending on the trimester. In the first trimester, straining to lift heavy-objects may trigger a miscarriage. In later trimesters, the risks only increase. Due to hormone changes during pregnancy, the ligaments in a woman's pelvic floor and joints loosen; this makes them more prone to damage and stress. A weakened pelvic floor can lead to big problems with incontinence (inability to control urination) or even potentially lead to the womb collapsing into the vagina (prolapse). Although some women are more at risk than overs, a general rule of thumb is to avoid heavy lifting altogether and get someone to help you.

9. **Some Types of Exercise**

Exercise is highly recommended for all pregnant women, but certain types should be avoided. The following exercises present a variety of risks and are not suitable for pregnant women:

- Anything that involves jumping, bouncing, or leaping.
- Exercises with jerky movements or sudden direction changes.
- Contact sports such as soccer, boxing, basketball, or ice hockey.
- Abdominal exercises that involve lying on the back.

- Exercises that require lying on the stomach.

- Activities with a fall risk such as rock-climbing, skiing, gymnastics, and horseback riding.

10. Certain Over-the-Counter Medications

Pregnant women are advised against taking medication they used before pregnancy unless they speak to a doctor about it first. Many seemingly harmless over-the-counter medications, such as aspirin or ibuprofen, are incredibly risky during pregnancy. In the first trimester, they can bring about miscarriage and later on, they can lead to birth defects in your baby. A good rule of thumb is to always talk to your doctor before you use any type of medicine.

The Truth About Weight Gain During Pregnancy

It is well-known that weight gain should be expected during pregnancy. While the amount of weight gained will vary from woman to woman, there are many who gain a tremendous amount of weight and unfortunately, this prospect can worry some new mothers. Of course, new mothers shouldn't worry about how much weight they're gaining; as long as they and their babies are healthy, that's all that matters. Still, it's completely understandable if some moms want to watch their weight and in some cases, it may be advised.

Most mothers will not be obese during their pregnancy, which is the only time weight gain can become a significant risk. Mothers who are obese are at an increased risk of preeclampsia, gestational diabetes, and premature birth. So if you were already overweight prior to becoming pregnant, pay close attention to the following facts.

- **You don't need extra calories in your first and second trimester**

We've all heard the phrase 'eating for two' used in conjunction with a pregnant woman, but unknown to most, this does not refer to the amount of food eaten. Pregnant women do not need to eat twice as much in the first and second trimester. It's not calories they need more of, but nutrients. Instead of eating larger amounts, they need to be focusing on more nutrient-rich foods. The misconception around 'eating for two' can lead to a lot of needless weight gain.

- **How much weight you need to gain depends on your starting weight**

The average woman needs to gain between 25 and 35 lbs for a healthy pregnancy but some may need to gain less or more, depending on how much they already weigh. The less you currently weigh, the more you'll need to gain and the more you weigh, the less you'll need to gain. Those who are underweight will need to gain between 28 and 40 lbs, while those who are overweight should only gain between 15 to 25 lbs. If you're pregnant with more than one baby, expect these numbers to be higher.

- **Weight is not just fat**

Weight gain is crucial for your pregnancy and that's because you're not just gaining fat. In fact, if a woman gains 35 lbs during pregnancy, only 5 to 9 lbs will consist of fat stores. Increased breast tissue, blood supply, uterus growth, amniotic fluid, the placenta, and of course, the baby itself all take up that extra weight. Putting on less weight could mean giving your baby less of what it needs to be completely healthy – so don't try to put on less than your recommended weight.

- **Weight gain isn't consistent**

You won't gain weight steadily throughout your pregnancy. You'll go many weeks remaining at a consistent weight but you'll also see times, usually in the second trimester, where weight gain happens very rapidly. And later in the third trimester, as you approach your due date, all weight gain will come to a halt.

- **Safe exercise can keep excess fat off**

Not only will it help with weight gain, but it can also relieve aches and pains during the latter part of pregnancy. The important thing is that exercise isn't too strenuous. The perfect way to stay active is by making walking a part of your routine. Doctors recommend starting with at least ten minutes of walking a day and adding ten minutes every month. And remember, the walking you do while running errands counts too! If you enjoyed jogging before you were pregnant, feel free to continue doing this.

What About Stretch Marks?

When skin stretches due to rapid weight gain, this can result in stretch marks. Over the course of pregnancy, women may get stretch marks on their belly, breasts, thighs, upper arms, and sometimes even on their buttocks. Fresh stretch marks often appear slightly red or purple but as they get older, they'll fade to a white or silver color.

Unfortunately, there is no sure way to avoid stretch marks completely. Nine out of ten women get them to some degree during pregnancy. Genetics will also play a big role in determining whether you get stretch marks and their appearance. If your parents or grandparents developed stretch marks, you're more likely to as well.

Even if you're genetically predisposed to get stretch marks, there are steps you can take to lower your chances. The following practices have proven to help with minimizing and preventing stretch marks:

Get Enough Vitamin D

Studies have shown that low levels of vitamin D can increase the likelihood of getting stretch marks. To increase your levels of this important vitamin, consider eating foods fortified with vitamin D (many types of cereal, milk or yogurt) or getting more sun exposure.

Stay Moisturized

Stretch marks are far more likely to appear on dry skin – so to stave them off, make sure to keep your skin moisturized. Consider using brands such as Mederma, Earth Mama, or Bio-Oil which have all been known to help with existing stretch marks as well as prevention.

Stay Hydrated

Moisturizing on the outside is one thing, but increasing your water intake and moisture-levels inside can be far more beneficial for stretch mark prevention. When your body is fully hydrated, your skin softens and is, therefore, much less prone to developing stretch marks. Women with dry skin will find it a lot more difficult to avoid scarring from weight gain.

Get Lots of Vitamin C

Stretch marks or not, vitamin C is known to be highly beneficial in the pursuit of healthy skin. This is because vitamin C plays a crucial role in your body's production of collagen – an important protein responsible for your skin's elasticity. To boost your levels of vitamin C, eat more fruit and veg or consider taking a vitamin C supplement.

Control Your Pregnancy Weight

A mother should never limit her nutrient intake in pursuit of being smaller-sized, but mothers *can* limit the amount of food they eat. Focus on small but frequent meals, rich with all the nutrients you need. And when you can, try to stave off cravings for unhealthy food!

Treat Stretch Marks as Soon as They Appear

The sooner you treat stretch marks, the higher the likelihood of improving their appearance. Once you see purple or red marks forming, make sure to lather on a reliable stretch mark-control product or moisturizer. For the best luck, you'll need to treat the affected area daily even if you don't see results as fast as you want to. Even those who moisturize diligently can end up waiting a month to see big improvements.

5 Health-Boosting Supplements for Mom and Baby

As soon as you become pregnant, your body starts to demand more nutrients. This is true of macronutrients such as protein, fat, and carbohydrates, but it is especially true for micronutrients, which include vitamins and minerals. To make sure you're meeting this growing demand, it's recommended that women either commit to eating a nutrient-rich diet or at the very least, make supplements a part of their daily routine. If you're experiencing strong aversions to food or nausea during your pregnancy, you're going to want to keep a stock of these supplements so you're still getting the nutrients you need.

In addition to these supplements, make sure you talk to your doctor about the best prenatal vitamins for you to take. Your prenatal vitamins will cover a decent chunk of your nutrient requirements, but not everything. It's always best to see what your prenatal vitamins give you and what you need to get most of elsewhere.

Please note that all the supplements on this list have been deemed safe by medical health professionals. If you're considering taking a supplement that is not on this list, speak to a doctor before doing so.

Folic Acid

Recommended Amount: 600 mcg

Natural Sources: Asparagus, eggs, beets, avocado, spinach, broccoli.

Vitamin B9, commonly known as Folic Acid, is well-known for being vital to a growing baby's development and overall health. Numerous studies have shown that folic acid is directly responsible for reducing the risk of certain birth defects and abnormalities. Doctors even recommend a folate supplement for women trying to get pregnant, as intake before pregnancy brings even more benefits. Although it is possible, most women do not eat enough folate through their diet alone so a supplement can help greatly.

Vitamin D

Recommended Amount: 50 mcg

Natural Sources: sunlight, fatty fish such as salmon or mackerel, egg yolks, foods fortified with vitamin D including dairy and some cereals.

Vitamin D deficiency is, unfortunately, very common, not just in pregnant women but all people. In pregnancy, an inadequate intake of vitamin D has been linked to bone fractures, abnormal bone growth, preeclampsia, bacterial vaginosis, and rickets in newborns. Vitamin D is an essential nutrient for all pregnant women as it plays a prominent role in building your baby's bones and teeth. Unlike most other vitamin deficiencies, it is possible to be vitamin D deficient and display no obvious symptoms.

Iron

Recommended Amount: 27 mg

Natural Sources: oysters, clams, mussels, chicken or beef liver, spinach.

Your maternal blood volume will increase by 50% during pregnancy, so this means your need for iron will as well. Iron has proven to be crucial in the healthy development of both the fetus and the placenta. Iron deficiency, or anemia, has been linked to a higher risk of infant anemia, preterm delivery and even depression for the mother-to-be. With iron, it's important that only the recommended intake is consumed and not more than that. Too much iron can induce vomiting, constipation, and many other unpleasant side effects.

Magnesium

Recommended Amount: 310 mg

Natural Sources: Dark chocolate, avocado, almonds, cashews, tofu, pumpkin seeds, flax seeds, spinach.

A woman's requirement for magnesium increases during pregnancy, and since it gets excreted in larger amounts through urine or vomiting (morning sickness), it is advised that mothers replenish their magnesium levels through their diet or supplementation. Studies have shown that a magnesium deficiency in pregnant women leads to a higher risk of preterm birth, preeclampsia, and fetal growth restriction. Sufficient levels, however, have been linked to reduced cramping while pregnant and, believe it or not, newborns with better sleep cycles!

Iodine

Recommended Amount: 260 mcg

Natural Sources: Cod, plain yogurt, cottage cheese, shrimp, eggs.

Our daily requirement for iodine is extremely tiny in comparison to other vitamins and minerals – but that tiny amount is very important. In pregnant women, iodine assists the thyroid in regulating hormones that control your heart rate, metabolism, and other functions. Mothers who do not get enough iodine significantly increase the risk of their baby being born with an underdeveloped thyroid. This can lead to a child with deafness, birth defects, learning disabilities, a low IQ, and much more. Since too much iodine can also pose serious risks, doctors recommend taking an iodine supplement with only 150 mcg and no more.

Before we dive into the first trimester, please keep in mind that everything in this chapter applies to the entire pregnancy. Make good habits part of your daily routine and eventually, both you and your baby will reap the benefits!

Chapter 2 - The First Trimester

Did you know the first trimester begins before you're even pregnant? Unknown to most, Day 1 is not the day of conception, but instead the first day of your last period before becoming pregnant. The first trimester lasts from this day until the end of week 12. When a woman discovers she is pregnant, she's usually five or six weeks into her pregnancy already. By this point, a heartbeat can usually be detected. Believe it or not, your baby grows the most rapidly in the first trimester than in any other trimester. More changes happen in such a short space of time than at any other point in your pregnancy. Curious about what these changes are? Here are some of the biggest developments of the first trimester:

- The fertilized egg has implanted itself into your womb – where it'll continue to grow for the next eight to nine months.

- The embryo will start dividing into three layers. The topmost layer will eventually form your baby's skin, eyes, and ears. The middle layer will become your baby's bones, kidneys, ligaments, and most of their reproductive system. And from the bottom layer, your baby's other organs such as the lungs and intestines will begin to develop.

- By the time week 12 rolls around, your baby's muscles and bones have formed, as well as all the organs of their body. It has a distinguishable human form and can now officially be called a fetus.

As these big developments take place, a mother's body starts to experience a lot of new feelings. You're likely going through some of these already. Rest assured, it's all part of the process that is the formation of life.

10 Common Symptoms of the First Trimester & How to Manage Them

You'll start feeling pregnant long before you start looking pregnant. It may be the early days but the first trimester is still fraught with its own set of symptoms. When you don't know what to expect, it can be difficult to distinguish between what's normal and what isn't. Not every mother will experience the symptoms on this list – in fact, you may even find that it varies with each pregnancy you have. If you're experiencing any of the following symptoms, know that it's completely normal and most mothers will tick off at least a box or two. And best of all, there is some degree of relief available.

1. **Morning Sickness**

There isn't just one cause for morning sickness, but it's largely due to rising hormone levels. Unfortunately, the term 'morning sickness' is rather misleading. Pregnancy-related nausea and vomiting can hit you at any time of the day, typically starting after week 6. As awful as you may feel, doctors do not advise skipping meals; in fact, you may find yourself feeling even worse on an empty stomach. Instead, just limit yourself to small meals, drink plenty of fluids, and sip on some stomach-soothing ginger tea. If nausea persists, consider getting some acupressure wristbands. Thankfully, morning sickness tends to subside by the second trimester.

2. **Fatigue**

Your body is making a lot of adjustments and changes to accommodate a baby, and naturally, this can result in extreme tiredness. Sometimes the best thing to do is to just let yourself relax and lay down, as you please. Now's the time for self-care. Curl up on the sofa and read, watch TV, or do whatever it is you enjoy doing in your spare time. If you're frustrated with being sedentary all the time, consider adding energy-boosting foods to your diet. Some of these include sweet potatoes, spinach, and oatmeal. And while you're at it, make sure you're drinking enough water as dehydration can add to pregnancy fatigue.

3. Constipation

It's normal to have more trouble than usual with bowel movements while pregnant. If you're not exercising or drinking enough water, this can contribute to the problem. It's also common knowledge that certain prenatal vitamins can make constipation even worse. If the problem persists after hydrating and exercising more often, you may want to speak to your doctor about switching to different vitamins.

4. Aversions to Certain Foods

Due to hormonal changes, you're likely to feel completely repulsed by certain foods. This is usually linked to feelings of morning sickness. Some of the foods you'll feel averse to may include spicy food, meat (especially red), garlic, milk and any others that give out a strong smell. The only way to manage this one is to be kind to yourself – if a certain food makes you feel sick, don't force yourself to eat it. You can find those nutrients in other foods. Have fun at the grocery store and pick out many different options for yourself. Once you're home, sort the ones that make you feel sick from the ones you can stand or actually like.

5. Food Cravings

And then you have the very opposite of food aversions – cravings! The feeling that you just gotta have it and you gotta have it *now*. For the most part, there's no harm in indulging your food cravings. However, it may become a problem if you're craving very specific foods all the time or your cravings are extremely unhealthy. Believe it or not, 30% of women report of craving non-food items such as soap or chalk. If you're experiencing non-food cravings, please do not satisfy these urges!

Before satisfying a craving, try drinking a tall glass of water first. It's actually surprisingly common to mistake thirst for hunger. Make sure you're not dehydrated before you rush to indulge. A second way to keep cravings at bay is by adding more protein to your diet. Studies have found a link between more protein at breakfast and the number of cravings throughout the day.

6. Frequent Urination

The need to frequently urinate can crop up as early as week 4 into your pregnancy – before you even know you're pregnant! Your kidneys need to become more efficient at getting rid of waste during your pregnancy, so this is an annoying side effect of extra blood flow going to your kidneys and pelvic area. Unfortunately, this symptom only becomes more extreme as pregnancy continues. Soon, your uterus will begin growing and so will your baby, increasing the amount of pressure on your bladder. There's no way to stop this altogether and it is highly advised that pregnant women do not minimize their water intake to attempt to control it. To avoid making it worse, limit your intake of coffee, tea, and soft drinks, which only increase the urgent need to urinate.

7. Tender and Swollen Breasts

Your body is preparing to provide nourishment to a baby and when the baby arrives, it'll need sustenance from your breasts. To prepare for this, your breasts will begin to grow and change – and this can result in skin that is tender or swollen. This starts in the first trimester and will continue throughout your entire pregnancy. If you're still using your pre-pregnancy bras, this may be exacerbating the issue. Give your breasts the support they need and consider purchasing a high-quality maternity bra. This may not solve the issue altogether but will definitely provide some relief.

8. Mood Swings

If you're feeling moody, restless, easily irritated, or just more down than usual, rest assured that it's completely normal. Depression and mood swings are common when your hormones are on overdrive. A key way to manage these symptoms is by making sure you're sleeping enough and eating a nutritious diet. Since your energy levels are already low, it's important you continue to recharge so your emotional wellbeing doesn't suffer. And always remember to make time for fun. If you're working while you're pregnant, make sure there's always time each day to devote to an activity that brings you joy.

9. Heartburn

During pregnancy, a woman produces higher levels of the hormone progesterone. This hormone has a soothing effect on certain muscles, including the ring of muscle in the esophagus. Unfortunately, when this muscle relaxes, it has a harder time keeping acids in your stomach, leading to acid reflux and – you guessed it – heartburn. To lower your chances of heartburn, doctors recommend avoiding spicy or acidic foods, eating smaller but more frequent meals, and waiting at least an hour before laying down after a meal. And to soothe heartburn, a glass of honey and milk or a small cup of yogurt can do wonders.

10. Skin Changes

You've likely heard of the 'pregnancy glow' where your cheeks get rosy and your entire complexion just seems a little brighter. Mothers-to-be tend to get the pregnancy glow in the first trimester, fairly early on. But unfortunately, not everyone will see positive changes. Some women will experience more oil than usual and this may even result in acne and breakouts. If you were prone to breakouts during your period, chances are that pregnancy will make you break out too. Thankfully, these skin changes are temporary and will subside once your hormones go back to normal. Whatever you do, steer clear of skin products with salicylic acid or vitamin A (retinol) unless you speak to a doctor first as these ingredients are known to affect pregnancy.

When to Call Your Doctor

You probably won't experience any big problems during your pregnancy, but it's always important to stay informed. If any of the following symptoms apply to you, call your doctor for additional help. It could indicate a more serious problem.

Heavy Vaginal Bleeding

Spotting is very common for pregnant women, but heavy bleeding is usually a cause for concern especially if there is any cramping or abdominal pain. In the early days, there is still a chance for a miscarriage or an ectopic pregnancy. Heavy bleeding can often be a signifier of one of these unfortunate complications.

Vaginal Discharge and Itching

It's completely normal to have some vaginal discharge during pregnancy – but look out for unusual discharge that's accompanied by itching. This could be a symptom of a sexually transmitted disease (STD). These are usually treatable but they can sometimes have negative effects on your pregnancy. If it's possible you have an STD, reach out to a doctor right away so it doesn't affect your baby.

Severe Nausea or Vomiting

Some level of morning sickness is an expected part of pregnancy, but if any of the following applies to you, contact your doctor.

- You vomit more than three times a day on most days.

- You've gone 12 hours without keeping down any liquid.

- You've thrown up blood, even if it's a small amount.

Urination with a Burning Sensation

Urinary Tract Infections (UTIs) are very common in pregnancy. While it's usually nothing to worry about, it becomes a more serious matter when you're pregnant. If left untreated, a UTI can cause a kidney infection, which has the potential to trigger a preterm birth or lead to a low birth-weight baby. Antibiotics from a doctor can easily solve the problem of a UTI, so it's essential mothers-to-be seek treatment for a fully preventable complication.

A High Fever

There are many potential causes for a high fever in pregnancy – while some of them are no cause for concern, it's important to rule out more serious causes. At its worst, it could be an infection, which may result in developmental complications in your growing baby. Even if you feel strongly that it's just a normal fever, doctors do not advise self-medicating since some pain-relieving medicines are dangerous during pregnancy. Be safe at any sign of a fever and call your doctor.

5 Ways Your Body Will Change in the First Trimester

As your body prepared to make a home for a baby, it will see a range of new changes and developments. While many of these will happen later on in the pregnancy, a good deal of changes will start as early as the first trimester.

1. **Your Breasts**

As your mammary glands increase in size, your breasts will swell to prepare for breastfeeding. Your areolas (the colored areas around your nipples) will also get darker and larger. For some women, the sweat glands in this area can also become larger, resulting in tiny, white bumps.

2. Vaginal Discharge

Pregnant women tend to get more vaginal discharge than they're used to. Normal discharge is milky with a thin consistency. Some women are more comfortable when they wear a small pad.

3. Hair Thickening

Many pregnant women report of thick and shiny hair that looks even healthier than it did before pregnancy. Unfortunately, this can also be accompanied by more hair growth on other areas of the body, such as the face, stomach, and sometimes even the back. You can thank rising estrogen levels for this!

4. Brittle Nails

Another side effect of higher estrogen levels is brittle nails. Many mothers find their nails are softer and more prone to splitting. It isn't all estrogen's fault, however; many experts think that increased blood flow in the toes and fingers could also be the culprit.

5. Bigger Feet

Don't worry, this doesn't happen to all women who get pregnant! Due to an increase in growth hormones, many mothers-to-be get bigger and sometimes flatter feet. It'll happen gradually over the course of your pregnancy. Believe it or not, some women have grown a whole shoe size!

What is a Doula & How Can They Help?

A birth doula is a trained professional whose primary job is to provide physical and emotional support to mothers over the course of their entire pregnancy. Although they can be hired at any time, including at the last minute, it's recommended that mothers hire a doula as early as possible, to allow more time for getting comfortable with your doula.

If you choose to hire a doula, she will assist you with the following:

- Breathing techniques, labor positions, and soothing through massage or other relaxation methods on the day of labor and delivery.

- Coaching and supporting the father (or other birth partner) so that they, too, can provide the best support for the new mother.

- Emotional support through the ups and downs of pregnancy, until the very end and perhaps even beyond.

- Letting you know whether you're in labor and when it's time to go to the hospital.

- Creating a more comforting environment for labor and delivery, e.g. with soft music, dim lights, candles, etc.

- Helping you to and from the bathroom (when needed) and making sure you've eaten and drunk enough on the day of delivery.

The contributions of a doula go far and wide, and many women claim they could never have done it without the help of one. This said, it's important to remember that a doula does not provide medical advice. Her assistance does not replace help from a doctor.

What Are the Benefits of Hiring a Doula?

Doulas have proven to have the following benefits on a mom and her pregnancy and childbirth experience:

- Significantly reduced anxiety.
- Decreases the time spent in labor by 25%.
- Less likely to need an epidural or other pain relief medication.
- Chances of needing a C-section lowered by 50%.
- Higher chances of breastfeeding success.
- A better bonding experience with the new baby.
- An overall more positive childbirth experience.

How Much Does a Doula Cost?

The cost of a doula varies widely and for some people, they may even be partially or completely covered by your health insurance provider. If you're paying out of pocket, expect a doula to cost between $800 and $2500.

Is a Doula Right for You?

As remarkable as a doula can be, not every mother feels she is the right fit for one – and that's totally okay! It all depends on your personality. Some women dislike the idea of someone they don't know being present during intimate moments. Keep in mind your doula will be there for some of your most difficult days. She will be getting up close and personal with you because that's the best way she can help. While most women find a doula's support empowering, others feel they get enough support from elsewhere.

If you have a very supportive and hands-on family with lots of pregnancy and childbirth experience, a doula may not be necessary. And if you take a long time to feel comfortable around a person you don't know well, your personality type may not be the right fit. But unless you fall into any of these categories, I've found that doulas are always incredible help. Many families stay in touch with their doulas because they gain a friend after the many months spent together. If you can afford it, consider a doula.

How Can I Find a Doula?

There are many ways to find the doula of your dreams. Try searching online directories such as:

- DONA International
- Birthing From Within
- Childbirth and Postpartum Professional Association (CAPPA)
- Doula Match

Choose the doula that suits your needs (in this case, you'd need a childbirth doula) and interview as many candidates as you can. You'll be spending a lot of time with this person so make sure that it's someone you feel comfortable with! And of course, always ensure that they have the right training and certifications. When you find the doula you're meant for, you'll get a good gut feeling!

For many moms, the first trimester is the most difficult – especially if you have some intense symptoms. Thankfully, some easier days are ahead. As moms transition into their next trimester, they find a lot of relief from their difficult symptoms.

Chapter 3 - The Second Trimester

Welcome to the second trimester! You're about halfway through the journey and you're probably incredibly relieved to reach this milestone. Many difficulties of the first trimester like morning sickness and fatigue will ease away in the second trimester. It's likely that you're feeling more energetic than you did and your breasts may even feel less tender. If you aren't feeling these positive developments yet, hold on! They'll get there soon enough.

In the first trimester, you will have gained little or no weight (unless you were very skinny) but this will change in the second trimester. Your belly will expand significantly in these next few months and you'll finally start to look pregnant. Since it's a period of rapid growth, this is when stretch marks are most likely to appear. You'll have more need for maternity clothes during this time, so make sure you're well-stocked with pregnancy wear that offers you comfort and support.

There's a lot happening inside your belly. Over the second trimester, these changes among many others begin to take effect:

- Your baby's organs are fully developed now.

- Your baby can hear! His or her first sounds will be the sound of your voice, the beating of your heart, the grumbling of your belly, and all the other fascinating noises of the human body.

- You'll finally be able to feel your baby moving around. This is more common later on in the second trimester.

Pelvic Floor Exercises that All Mothers Must Know

Now that you're more settled into your pregnancy, it's time to work on strengthening your pelvic floor muscles. This is a completely optional practice and will have no bearing whatsoever on your baby – but mothers who strengthen their pelvic floor are always relieved they did. This practice is just for the benefit of mom!

During pregnancy and birth, a woman's pelvic floor is stretched beyond its usual limits. These muscles are responsible for keeping the bladder closed and controlling urine that goes out or stays in. When the pelvic floor muscles become weakened, a woman is more likely to leak urine accidentally, especially while sneezing, coughing, or straining in some way. Since these muscles also help keep the anus closed, there may even be less control over breaking wind.

Unfortunately, pelvic floor muscles do not get stronger on their own. To avoid the embarrassing moments listed, women must make the effort to strengthen their pelvic muscles and better yet, make these exercises part of their routine. Some of these exercises may feel difficult to do at first but with practice, you'll get the hang of them. Just as other muscles in your body can get stronger, so can your pelvic floor.

Isolating the Pelvic Floor Muscles

This is an essential first step and one that is best tried while sitting on the toilet. While urinating, stop the flow midstream. The muscles you've just activated are your pelvic floor muscles. See if you can stop yourself from urinating for two seconds and then continue emptying your bladder as normal. It's important to note that this is not a pelvic floor exercise; this is just a way to help beginners identify the pelvic floor muscles. It is not recommended to habitually stop urination midstream. If you find yourself tightening your buttocks while trying to isolate these muscles, then you haven't yet succeeded. It's okay – just keep trying!

Once you've identified your pelvic floor muscles, you're ready to start exercising them. If you're a beginner, it may be best to empty your bladder completely first. And a word of caution: stick to the reps listed and do not over-exercise – or you may find this practice backfiring.

- **Exercise #1**

This beginner's exercise can be performed anywhere, at any time. Tighten the muscles in your pelvic floor and hold them for ten seconds. Then, relax the muscles for ten seconds. Perform ten repetitions, three to five times a day.

- **Exercise #2**

Get into a sitting position and imagine that you're sitting on a marble. Next, tighten the muscles in your pelvic floor as if you're pulling that marble upwards. Imagine lifting the marble with your pelvic floor alone. Hold the marble for three seconds and then release it for three seconds. Perform ten to fifteen repetitions, three times a day.

- **Exercise #3**

Instead of holding the marble for three seconds, try only holding it for one second. To do this faster-paced exercise, pull the imaginary marble upwards quickly, lift it, and immediately release. Perform these fast contractions as well as the slower ones a few times a day.

5 Ways to Start Bonding With Your Baby

Although you can start bonding with your baby at any time, the second trimester is an especially wonderful time to do it. As I mentioned at the beginning of this chapter, your baby can now hear you. This opens up many more ways to bond with your little one. Here are some ways you can start bonding now:

1. **Sing to Your Bump**

Your baby knows your voice extremely well by now. Since its the main voice he or she hears, it has become a very soothing sound and vibration. Sing a song or melody you love and send that positivity inside your belly. Your baby will enjoy being soothed in this way.

2. Talk to Your Baby

If you're not much of a singer, then don't stress. Your baby likes your voice regardless of whether it's in tune or not. To bond through the sound of your voice, try talking directly to your baby instead. Tell him or her how excited you are to meet or what the best parts of your day were.

3. Respond to Kicks

This method of bonding can be very fun. The next time your baby kicks, rub or massage the spot where you felt the kick. Some mothers even find that the baby will kick again. A back-and-forth can ensue – almost like a conversation!

4. Self-Care

Taking care of your mind and body used to just mean taking care of *you*. With a baby on board, however, you're taking care of two people. During acts of self-care, you'll instantly feel more calm and at peace – and this means your baby will get the message too. The next time you take a warm bath or get massaged, both you and your baby can bond through the soothing and relaxing sensations.

5. Prenatal Yoga

Not only will prenatal yoga allow you to get good exercise, but it's also a great opportunity to feel close to your little bump. As you pay attention to your breath and keep an open awareness of the being inside you, your baby will instantly feel at peace. Overall, prenatal yoga has some very positive effects on a mother-to-be's wellbeing.

Watch Out For These Signs of Preeclampsia

During a woman's first pregnancy, her risk of developing preeclampsia is at its highest. This risk is raised even higher if she is obese, very young or older than 40, carrying more than one baby, conceived through in vitro fertilization or if she has a family history of preeclampsia

The major risk of preeclampsia is that it eventually leads to a life-threatening complication, such as organ damage, placental abruption or eclampsia – a very serious condition where both mom and baby are at risk of death. Unfortunately, the only way to cure preeclampsia is by delivering the baby and oftentimes, preeclampsia strikes when a baby is too young to be delivered. At this point, the new mother is left with a difficult decision: risk two lives and carry the baby to term or abort the pregnancy. Since preeclampsia can start as soon as 20 weeks into a pregnancy, it's important that you pay attention to your body's changes in the second trimester.

The symptoms of preeclampsia are:

- High blood pressure in pregnant women who have never before had high blood pressure.

- Sudden swelling in the face, eyes or hands – though keep in mind that ankle and feet swelling is completely normal during pregnancy.

- Rapid weight gain, especially over a few days.

- Severe headaches.

- Vision changes such as blurry vision, temporary loss of vision or sensitivity to light.

- Reduced urination or no urination at all.

- Excessive nausea and vomiting.

- Abdominal pain, especially if it occurs in the upper right side.

- Severe shortness of breath.

Your routine prenatal visits will keep track of potential preeclampsia signs. But since many of these symptoms can come on suddenly, it's essential that you seek help as soon as they arise. Do not take chances with preeclampsia symptoms.

The Best Ways to Exercise in the Second Trimester

You're starting to expand and you're likely wondering how you can get some safe exercise. The good news is that you can still do most of the activities you were doing in the first trimester. As long as exercise isn't strenuous and doesn't come with a fall risk, it's probably safe to do. Here are some of the most popular methods of exercise among pregnant women in the second trimester:

1. Swimming

No matter the trimester, whether it's the early days or late in the third trimester, swimming is one of the best ways for a pregnant woman to exercise. Not only is it incredibly safe (with absolutely zero fall-risk) and low-impact but many women find it soothing on their aches and pains. If you'd like to incorporate swimming into your exercise routine, just make sure to avoid strokes that require you to twist your middle-section and abdomen around. Go for 15-30 minute sessions (depending on how much you swam before you became pregnant) at least three times a week. If you're a more experienced swimmer, it is safe to do it daily.

2. Yoga

Remember when I said yoga is a great way to bond with your baby? It's also just a great form of exercise for all preggo moms. Yoga allows mom to breathe and stretch out her sore muscles, reducing the aches and pains of pregnancy. It can also teach her breathing techniques that may be beneficial later on during labor. To stay 100% safe, doctors advise sticking to gentle positions and avoiding poses like the Tree or Warrior which make it more possible for mom to fall over. And steer clear of poses that require you to lie on your back or twist at the waist. Hot yoga is also strongly discouraged during pregnancy.

3. Walking

Walking is always safe during pregnancy, so rest assured that if all other exercises fail, a good and leisurely walk will do the trick. Experts even recommend trying to engage the arms as you walk; this can build strength and flexibility in your upper body. For the best exercise, walk at a faster pace to get your heart rate a little higher. As long as you're free from a fall-risk (no difficult hiking!), this is completely safe for mom and baby. This is also true for women who are heavily pregnant.

4. Light Jogging

Light jogging and running are only recommended if you did this before you got pregnant. If you used to jog before, feel free to try a toned-down version of your previous routine. The most important thing is that you pay attention to your body and immediately stop running if you feel any back or joint pain. Fall-risk is also a concern with this exercise, so experts recommend only running on a treadmill with reliable safety features or a flat, unbroken sidewalk. Women who are not used to jogging or running are not advised to start doing it now.

10 Fun Ideas for the Second Trimester

If I had to choose the trimester I enjoy the most, it's by far the second trimester. With so many difficult pregnancy symptoms out of the way, you can finally embrace and enjoy being pregnant. No more nausea means food is wonderful again. No more fatigue means you can finally get some stuff done and feel good about it. You're at that perfect middle point. Here are some of my favorite fun second-trimester activities.

1. Have a Gender Reveal Party

Most women find out the gender of their baby in the second trimester. Know what this means? It's the perfect time for a gender reveal party! Gather your friends and family to celebrate the unveiling of your baby's gender. Many people enjoy filming the reactions of both parents to learning this exciting new detail about their baby. If you're interested in throwing a gender reveal party, there are a number of fun reveal ideas! Consider a gender reveal cake, balloon pop, confetti, or if you're feeling wild, fireworks!

2. Announce Your Pregnancy Publicly

Announcing a pregnancy in the first trimester is always risky since the chance of a miscarriage happening is highest at that point. Once you're in the second trimester, however, you can finally safely make the announcement! Whether you're holding a gender reveal party or not, you can have fun with your announcement to your wider group of friends on family. An adorable social media post or a beautiful card are some ideas you can use. What an exciting time!

3. Go on a Babymoon

If you've ever wanted a second honeymoon, now's your chance! The second trimester is a great time to enjoy your final vacation before having a kid. By the time the third trimester rolls around, you'll find that most airlines won't let you fly internationally, so now's the time to get your international travel fix. If you don't have the time or money for a big vacation, then why not see a different part of the country or have a staycation? Whatever form it takes, you and your partner should absolutely enjoy your last months as a child-free couple.

4. Go on a Shopping Spree for Maternity Clothes

You're going to see some significant weight gain in the second trimester and that means it's time for some new clothes. Go maternity shopping by yourself or with some other pregnant friends. And for the best selection, look online. Treat yourself to new clothes that make you feel fantastic about your new body. Many new moms prefer more fitted clothes to baggy clothes; this allows them to embrace their new curves, making them instantly feel more sexy. You deserve to feel good, first-time mom!

5. Buy Some Lingerie to Restart the Fire in the Bedroom

If you're feeling a little more sensual than usual, you can thank your fluctuating hormones! Enjoy these feelings and bring your partner into the mix to enjoy them too. If you're so inclined, throw in some new lingerie the next time you go maternity clothes shopping. You'll get a lot bigger in the third trimester so now's the time to get lingerie you can still wear after you're pregnant!

6. Have a Maternity Photoshoot

Flaunt your new body and feel beautiful! Maternity photoshoots are not about vanity; it's about commemorating a beautiful time in your life. As a first-time mom, how wonderful would it be to make memories if your experience in the form of gorgeous photographs? The second trimester is perfect as you look pregnant enough for a maternity shoot but you're not big enough to start getting self-conscious. Browse online for a good maternity photographer or ask for referrals from friends. It may sound like a wild idea but many mothers deeply cherish these photos! Feel free to get your partner involved as well.

7. Incorporate Gentle Exercise into your Routine

Now that you're in the second trimester, you've likely gotten your energy back. Without the fatigue to hold you back, it's a great time to start getting into gentle exercise. Take a look at the previous section and find an exercise method that you like best! If you weren't very fit before you got pregnant, take it easy as you're not any fitter now that you're expecting. Always listen to your body!

8. Decorate and Furnish the Nursery

When your baby arrives, you'll want to have the nursery completely ready. If you're planning on having it painted, it's especially important that there aren't any lingering paint fumes. Get the essentials out of the way in the second trimester while you have the energy to decorate and furnish. The bigger you get, the less time you're going to want to spend on your feet. If paint and chemicals need to be handled, get your partner to take over this job and make sure you aren't inhaling any dangerous fumes.

9. Interview More Doulas

If you haven't decided on a doula or are making last minute decisions about having one, now's the time to get serious about the search. Doulas can be hired at any time but the earlier you have one on board, the more help they can offer. Interview more doula candidates and have one decided on before your second trimester ends. It's totally possible to have fun with this! Many doulas end up forming a friendship with the family, so you can even try to see this as interviewing a potential new family friend. Get to know these candidates and laugh with them. If you're still struggling to find a childbirth doula, search for them online or ask other mothers you know for referrals.

10. Take a Childbirth Class

It's not too late to take a childbirth class. If you didn't attend one in your first trimester, consider doing it now. Mothers who make the time to take these classes are always glad they did – and some birthing centers even require you to take them! The information you'll glean is invaluable. Another bonus? You'll meet other first-time moms, the perfect allies on this crazy ride! Connecting with other first-time moms is one of the best things you can do for yourself. When both your babies are born, you can empower each other and help each other learn. When you're done with childbirth class, consider taking others on breastfeeding or newborn care.

Chapter 4 - The Third Trimester

You're finally in the home stretch of your pregnancy the third and last trimester. This trimester is easily the most exciting as it ends with the ultimate reward: bringing your baby out into the world and getting to hold him or her in your arms. Keep in mind that, although you may have a due date set, there's a chance your baby will arrive sooner than you expect. It's important that you recognize the signs you're going into labor, as soon as they arise. But before we get into that, here's a quick rundown on how your baby is continuing to develop in these final months:

- Your baby's eyelashes have formed and he or she is now capable of opening their eyelids.

- It's finally happened! Your baby can kick! He or she can also stretch and gently grasp.

- Hair has grown – and if you have thick hair genes, it's possible your baby is starting to develop a fantastic head of hair.

- What a little cutie – your baby's skin is now smooth and taking on a chubby appearance.

To sum up, your baby is finally starting to resemble a full-on tiny human. Your body is putting the finishing touches on the child you'll soon hold in your arms. In the meantime, however, there's a lot to do to prepare for his or her arrival.

Every First-Time Mom's To-Do List for the Third Trimester

1. **Finish Your Baby's Nursery**

As soon as your little bundle comes home from the hospital, you'll want to have his or her nursery ready to be slept in. This means you'll need a cot. If you plan on painting the nursery, get this done as soon as possible so that your baby does not have to be exposed to the smell of paint – which can be harmful if exposure lasts for more than a brief moment.

2. Prepare Everything Your Baby Will Need

When your baby comes, the last thing you'll want to do is rush to the store. Both you and your partner will want to enjoy every second of being with your newborn – any interruption would be extremely annoying! The third trimester is the perfect time to stock up on your baby's essentials so you don't need to run out for them later. You'll need diapers, blankets, newborn onesies, and much more. Get the full list in the following chapter.

3. Read as Much as You Can

This new chapter of your life is like no other chapter you've known before. This is why it's strongly encouraged for all mothers to fully inform themselves about how to properly care for a child. Thankfully for all mothers, there's a lot of information out there, easily accessible to all. In fact, by reading this book, you're already making strides towards being a fully prepared mom! Still, you shouldn't stop at one book. Absorb as much information as you can from as many sources as possible.

4. Make Self-Care a Priority

You're carrying a child and your body deserves all the love it can get. Do everything you can to avoid strain and needless stress. Actively practice self-care. Pamper yourself with a prenatal massage at a great spa and when you're feeling tired, sit in bed and enjoy your favorite TV show. Do whatever makes you feel great. And keep in mind that self-care sometimes means doing something that is good for you, even if you don't really feel like doing it. Sure, treat yourself to a chocolate milkshake if it brings you joy, but more often than not, care for yourself by seeking out more nutritious options. To operate from a mindset of self-care, consider what your body really needs at that moment to create the best emotional environment for your baby.

5. Start a Baby Registry

There's no reason you should buy all the essentials yourself! Baby registries allow parents-to-be to list all items they need when their baby arrives. This, then, allows friends and family to give these items as gifts. Consider making your own baby registry on Amazon, Bed Bath & Beyond or Target.

6. Stock Your Freezer

With a new baby around, new parents tend to have a lot less energy for their regular cook-ups. Still, that's no excuse to neglect your hungry bellies and nutrient intake. You're going to need those calories! The third trimester is the perfect time to stock your freezer with microwavable meals or anything that doesn't require more than two steps to prepare. Pack as much in as you can. Neither you nor your partner will want to head out to the grocery store with a new little baby. If you prefer home-cooked meals, then an alternative is to cook your own meals to freeze for later.

7. Clean the House

This may seem like a strange to-do activity, but trust me, you'll be glad you did it when your baby comes. A surprising number of moms wish they'd cleaned up their home before their baby's arrival. Once the little bundle comes, there's simply no time or energy to deal with a messy house. Whether you do it with a partner or hire someone else to do it, try and get your home spic-and-span and mess-free before your big day.

8. Rest!

Once mothers enter the third trimester, it gets a little more difficult to sleep. No matter what you do, you just can't seem to get as comfortable as you used to. Nevertheless, it's important that moms get as much rest as they can. With childbirth on the horizon and exhausting days with a newborn baby looming, now's the time to try and get some much needed rest. It won't just be you and your partner for long! Make the most of the time you have to stay horizontal for as long as you like.

9. Decide Whether to Breast or Bottle-feed

To breastfeed or formula-feed – that is the question. Or at least, it is *one of* the questions of the third trimester. If you haven't decided yet, it's about time you do so. Why? Because very soon you'll need to start shopping to prepare for your new baby. And breastfeeding and bottle-feeding moms need slightly different equipment. If you're still feeling indecisive, let's examine the advantages of both options.

Breastfeeding vs. Formula Feeding

Breast

- When it comes to the nutrition factor, breast really is best. Mothers pass antibodies through their breast milk, meaning that their child is more resistant to certain illnesses and infections, such as meningitis and ear infections.

- Breast milk is easier to digest than other options. This means there's a much lower chance of your baby getting gassy or constipated.

- Breastfeeding is the least expensive option. You will need to buy formula but breast milk is, as you know, completely free. The money you spend on formula will quickly add up but breastfed babies just not you, a breast pump, bottles, and very few other supplies.

- Studies have shown there is some link between breastfeeding and babies with high levels of intelligence, i.e. cognitive function.

- Breastfeeding is also great for mothers. There is evidence that breastfeeding mothers have a lower risk of getting breast cancer, diabetes, ovarian cancer and more.

- Experts aren't so sure why but there appears to be a connection between breastfed babies and a reduced risk for Sudden Infant Death Syndrome (SIDS). Babies who are breastfed for at least six months are much less likely to die in their sleep.

- When breastfeeding happens regularly, it can burn up to 500 calories per day. If you're interested in shedding weight quickly after pregnancy, breastfeeding can help greatly.

Formula

- Formula feeding is far more convenient for mothers. Formula can be fed at any time and there is no need to take time out of your schedule to pump milk. This means your partner can feed the baby at any time, without needing help from you first.

- Babies don't digest formula as quickly as they digest breast milk, so there will be far more time between formula-feeds as opposed to breastfeeds. In other words, your baby will not need to be fed as often.

- There's no need to restrict your diet in any way. Babies that consume breast milk are very affected by what their mother eats and drinks, but with a formula-fed baby, mom can have whatever she likes. Foods and drinks that mothers should avoid while breastfeeding include hot spices, citrus fruits, alcohol, and anything with a high amount of caffeine. For the full list, see Chapter 8.

Tackling Third-Trimester Insomnia

As I mentioned previously, insomnia in the third trimester is not uncommon, especially for first-time moms. A number of factors contribute to this inability to sleep, from frequent urination and body pains to simply feeling huge and not being able to get comfortable. All new moms need their precious sleep; here are some helpful tips for fighting pregnancy insomnia.

1. **Invest in a high-quality pregnancy pillow.** You can find these in most maternity stores and they will work wonders for your sleep routine. Pregnancy pillows provide the perfect amount of support for mom so she can finally get in a comfortable position. Doctors actually recommend that pregnant women sleep on their left side after week 20, as this allows more blood flow to get to your baby. A pregnancy pillow is designed to make this position more comfortable.

2. **Make light exercise part of your routine.** As much as moms hate to hear it at this point in their pregnancy, a little daily exercise can help greatly. It may be difficult but try to get up and about at least once a day – it'll make you sleepier at night. Just try not to do it too close to your bedtime or you'll be buzzing with energy.

3. **Wear loose and comfortable nightwear.** Steer clear of tight-fitting clothing and stick to light materials like cotton that

allow your body to breathe. And if sleeping in the nude is the most comfortable for you, then why not? Do whatever you need to get sleep, first-time mom.

4. **Use as many pillows as you need.** This is especially important if you can't afford a pregnancy pillow. Get all the cushions and pillows in your home together (though you should probably leave at least one for your partner!) and experiment with as many arrangements and configurations as you can. Remember that sleeping on your left side is best for your baby right now. To mimic the support of a pregnancy pillow, try putting a cushion under your belly and between your knees.

5. **Sleep wherever you get comfortable.** If it's on your living room sofa or in an armchair, go for it. It doesn't have to be in your bed. Wherever you find yourself drifting off, allow yourself to just fall asleep. Sleep is hard to come by so take it whenever it comes.

6. **Fully hydrate by the early evening.** This way, you'll cut down on the number of times you need to go to the bathroom in the middle of the night and you'll still get all the water you need. Start hydrating as soon as you get up and stop drinking water when the evening rolls in.

7. **Get help from your doctor.** Thing is, some sleep medications and aids are perfectly fine to have while pregnant – but you should never go on them without telling your doctor first. If no other methods work, feel free to ask your doctor for more serious relief. He or she will be able to prescribe a sleep aid that is safe for your baby and exactly what you need.

Labor Signals & What They Mean

Natural birth or C-section, it's vital that every mother-to-be recognizes when they're going into labor. Even if your due date isn't for a few more weeks, it's always possible to have a premature baby. Each mother is going to have a slightly different experience during the weeks or days before labor sets in, but here are some of the many signals you're likely to experience and what they mean.

- **Your Baby Has 'Dropped'**

When the baby starts to sink lower into the pelvis, this is a key sign that the body is preparing for labor. But hold up, this doesn't necessarily mean that you're on the verge. A baby drop can happen as early as a month before labor.

- **An Increase in Back Pain and Cramping**

As your body prepared for birth, your joints and muscles with shift around and stretch. Unfortunately, this means more back pain and cramping for mom. While this is certainly a sign that labor is coming somewhat soon, there is no need to rush to the hospital. This signal means labor is as far as a month away and soon as a few days away.

- **Bloody Show**

In late pregnancy, thick vaginal discharge mixed with mucus and blood gets released by the vagina. This pink-hued discharge is called the 'bloody show' and it's a sign that the cervix is preparing for labor. The bloody show can indicate that labor is anywhere from a few weeks to a few hours away. If it's accompanied by other signals on this last, then labor may be close.

- **Your Water Breaks**

The water break is one of the last signs of labor a woman will experience. In other words, if it happens to you, you're most certainly in labor and your baby is on the way soon. Movies have misled people into thinking a public water break is common – but in reality, a premature break rarely happens. For most women, the water break happens well into labor and sometimes even moments before the baby actually emerges.

- **Contractions**

During labor, intense contractions are known to precede the time of delivery, but false-alarm contractions do exist. And this can confuse matters for many women. Braxton Hicks contractions are not labor contractions. Instead, they signal that the body is getting ready or warming up. There are many ways to tell Braxton Hicks contractions from Labor contractions, the most notable difference being that real contractions get more intense and closer together. When this is felt, you're most definitely in labor!

Braxton Hicks Contractions vs. Labor Contractions

Even though we've covered one way to distinguish between a false-alarm and real labor contraction, there are other signifiers too. No one wants to drag themselves all the way to the hospital just to be told to go home again – so let's make sure you understand these key differences! Here's how to know whether you're truly in labor or not:

Intensity

Braxton Hicks - These contractions are usually mild in intensity, without much variation in strength. Many women have also experienced them as strong to start with but weaker over time.

Labor - Contractions that indicate real labor have nowhere to go but up in intensity. They only get stronger and stronger over time.

Pain

Braxton Hicks - Pain is located on the front of your body, in your lower abdomen.

Labor - Pain exists in both the abdomen and the back. Some women even report that pain is *more* extreme in the back of the body. This is because the whole body prepares for real labor, not just one side.

Timing

Braxton Hicks - There is no discernible pattern between contractions. They come on seemingly at random with no specific regularity. They do not become more frequent.

Labor - Contractions come regularly and get closer together.

Adjustments

Braxton Hicks - Contractions stop or weaken with a change of position such as sitting, laying down, or walking.

Labor - It doesn't matter what you do, labor contractions still continue.

How Do You Induce Labor Safely and Naturally?

For labor to happen, two hormones are needed – prostaglandins and oxytocin. These two hormones trigger contractions and help to expand the cervix so that a baby can emerge. The key to inducing labor mostly revolves around trying to stimulate these hormones and therefore, labor. While many 'old wives tales' exist around the use of certain herbs, studies have not yet been performed to prove their efficiency or safety. Furthermore, many people suggest castor oil as a way to induce labor. I can confirm this method *does work*, but I highly discourage using it as it is also a laxative. Mothers who use castor oil end up going into labor dehydrated and with diarrhea. Do not make labor harder on yourself!

It is also extremely important to note that no one should try to induce labor unless they are due or past their due date. Inducing labor before your time should not be done unless a doctor gives you the OK.

- **Nipple Stimulation**

Let's make one thing clear: this type of nipple stimulation is not sexual at all! For this method to be successful, stimulation needs to mimic the suckling of a baby. Doing this will release oxytocin in the brain and may result in your uterus contracting, therefore beginning the process of labor.

- **Membrane Sweeping or Stripping**

If you're desperate, membrane sweeping is always an option – though it must be performed by your doctor. Using a gloved finger, your doctor will reach inside you to separate the amniotic sac from an area just inside the cervix. This releases prostaglandins and stimulates contractions to induce labor. Expect some discomfort during this procedure.

- **Having Sex**

It's important to note that sex doesn't always work at inducing labor. Still, there's a chance it might. Not only does sex release prostaglandins but male ejaculate also contains it. If the man ejaculates inside the vagina, it's possible the cervix will wake up and start contracting.

- **Eating Dates**

This method will not induce labor instantly, but if you start a few weeks before pregnancy, you may never have to induce labor. Studies have shown that eating 60-80 grams of dates per day in late pregnancy can reduce the need for induction and improve labor overall. Women who ate dates regularly decreased the length of the first stage of labor to almost half the time of women who didn't.

Chapter 5 - Preparing for the Big Day

When the big day arrives, the last thing you want to be is unprepared. No matter the type of birth you're having, there are a variety of ways you can and should make yourself more comfortable. Just a little prep can go a long way. Unprepared first-time mothers find themselves far more stressed and uncomfortable when the big moment arises – so avoid this, now that you have the choice. Follow these simple steps and you'll have everything you need to devote your full attention to you and your baby.

Pack These 13 Essentials in Your Hospital Bag

There's a possibility your little one will come knocking sooner than you think – so start packing your hospital bag just in case! Mothers who pack at the last minute (or allow someone to do it for them!) have admitted to ending up with a lot of useless stuff they didn't really need and without the stuff they really *did* need. The birth of your first child will be such a special time and the last thing you want is to be inconvenienced by something you could have prepared for.

1. **Your Daily Toiletries**

What essential toiletries are part of your morning and nighttime routine? Pack travel-sized versions in your bag. A stay at the hospital is no reason to neglect your self-care; in fact, it's a bigger reason to make it a priority. Bring your toothbrush, toothpaste, deodorant, and whatever else makes you feel cozy and at home. For efficiency and ease, consider getting some cleansing facial wipes instead of your usual face wash.

2. **Hair Ties and Clips**

The last thing you want is your hair getting in your face while you're giving birth. Pack hair ties and/or clips to keep your hair pulled back so you can focus on the big task without any minor annoyances.

3. Snacks and Drinks

This one is easily overlooked. It's not that food and drink aren't available where you'll be, it's more about the fact that mom and dad often want to stay together. Swept up in the special moment, it isn't uncommon for dad to opt for staying with mom instead of going off wandering for food. Without snacks readily available, many new parents can forget it's been several hours since their last meal.

4. Lip Balm

Have something that keeps your lips moisturized. Many mothers find their lips get chapped as they endure the intense hard work of labor. Keep those lips hydrated!

5. Comfortable Shoes

Ideally, these should be easy to slip on and off as you may want to do some walking around the hospital. Avoid all shoes that require you to bend over and/or strain in any way to get them on.

6. Pillows

Every hospital will provide pillows but don't expect them to be as comfortable as the ones you have at home. To ensure you're as comfortable as possible during this special but physically challenging time, bring your favorite pillow from home. Your partner may also want to bring a pillow as well.

7. A Dark-Colored Bathrobe or Dressing Gown

Whether it's in early labor or the postnatal ward, you're definitely going to be up and about in the hospital at some point. Make sure you're warm and comfortable by bringing something to wear over your hospital clothes. If you're worried about stains showing, pack something that's dark-colored.

8. Entertainment

Since mom will be preoccupied most of the time, this is more of a 'need' for dad. Pack something that can provide entertainment for many hours. This could be a book, a magazine, a music player, or something else. Whatever it is, make sure that it doesn't stress out or overwhelm mom!

9. Loose Clothes

Bring comfortable clothes, not just for the hospital but for your first ride home with your baby. It's important that you're not wearing anything too tight as you'll feel tender after delivery. Pack clothes that open easily at the front. This way, you'll be able to feed your baby with no difficulty as soon as the need arises.

10. Postpartum Underwear

Many first time moms get the mistaken impression that the hospital will supply them with proper underwear. Those who don't get *that* mistaken impression instead wrongly assume that it's fine to bring the underwear they wear normally. For starters, do *not* bring underwear that you would be upset to ruin. You will bleed heavily after giving birth and you'll need something that is up to the task. Get high-quality postpartum underwear that provides support, protection, and comfort.

11. Eyeglasses

This only applies to you if you wear them, of course. New mothers tend to not want to deal with their contact lenses when they're giving birth at a hospital. Since labor can take a while and it's possible you may be in and out of sleep, glasses tend to be the easier option. This may be down to personal preference. But if you're having a C-section, keep in mind you will be asked to remove your contact lenses beforehand.

12. Everything You Need to Be Photo-Ready

For some moms, this may mean nothing at all – but others might like to bring some mascara or powder to look a little less worn out in photos. This is completely up to mom and her preferences. Your partner and family members are likely excited to document the special day so bring any clothes or makeup you need to feel wonderful.

13. Massage Oil or Lotion

During the hours before labor or even after birth, many moms find massage incredibly soothing. Kick this up a notch by bringing a massage oil or lotion with a fragrance you find pleasant.

22 New-Baby & First-Time Mom Necessities

Of course, preparation is not just about the hospital visit and childbirth. It's also about that other special day – the day you get to bring your little one home. As soon as you get home, you'll need to have everything ready. Aside from a fully finished nursery with a crib or bassinet, you'll also need your child's smaller necessities. Take note of the following essentials; if you don't get them through your baby registry, get them yourself as soon as you can.

1. Diapers

Your newborn is gonna be one heck of a pooper – there's no way to avoid it! Needless to say, you're going to need diapers and a lot of them. Every mom can take their pick of disposable or cloth diapers.

- Disposable

Pros: *Most convenient option, more absorbent, less time-consuming.*

Disposable diapers are still a wildly popular option and it's no wonder why. The toss-when-you're-done approach is very convenient and requires no extra cleaning from mom or dad. But be prepared to spend more money in the long run – on average, parents who use disposables spend upwards of $2000 over two years. Not only this but the total amount of diapers used will create a lot of non-biodegradable waste for the environment. If you prefer the ease of disposable diapers, consider getting eco-friendly products from companies like *Honest*.

- Cloth

Pros: *Much cheaper in the long run, adjustable, kinder to sensitive skin, irritation less likely, reusable, eco-friendly.*

Over recent years, cloth diapers have become more widely used. Not only is it a money-saving option but cloth diapers today are far more effective than they used to be, thanks to innovation around eco-friendly baby products. To safeguard against potential skin irritation, cloth diapers are the way to go since absorbent chemicals in disposables can cause bad skin reactions for some babies. However, all parents who choose this route should keep in mind that cloth diapers require a lot more effort and time. Once your batch of diapers has been soiled, they'll need to be deep cleaned.

2. **One-Piece Baby Clothes**

Save the cute two-pieces for when your baby is a tiny bit older. To start off, focus on onesies or one-piece clothing that is easy to put on and take off. Since babies are extremely messy, you'll need to change your baby's clothes many times a day – keep this in mind when choosing clothes! Ideally, these garments should snap open at the bottom so you can do a diaper change with minimal hassle.

3. Mittens

If the onesies you've purchased don't cover your newborns hands, then some mittens will serve your newborn well. These are to ensure they don't scratch themselves with their little nails. Just two pairs should do the trick.

4. Baby Wipes

Try to get baby wipes that are suitable for more sensitive skin. Although your baby may not need a sensitive solution, it is always best to be safe with a newborn. These wipes will be used to clean your baby's bottom half during changing. On these sensitive areas, more care is needed.

5. Receiving Blankets

These multi-purpose blankets can be used for a myriad of things and they'll be your best friends in the months to come. Receiving blankets are soft, made of thin cotton, and usually come in a pack of three or four. Not only will these blankets provide your baby with comfort and warmth, but they also make great burping cloths, playmats, and feeding blankets for if you want more privacy during public breastfeedings.

6. Burp Cloths

As the name suggests, burp cloths are for covering clothes and wiping up spills, in the event that your baby spits up. And believe me, it will happen a lot. Receiving blankets can make handy substitute burp cloths but traditional burp cloths are much smaller and easier to carry around. While that extra surface area can be nice, it's not always entirely necessary.

7. Swaddling Blankets

To keep your baby comfortable and fully supported, you'll want to tuck him or her into a swaddling blanket. Again, a receiving cloth can be used as one, but real swaddling blankets are larger in size, more stretchy, and oftentimes, specially designed so that mom and dad can swaddle their baby with minimal hassle.

8. A Baby Carrier

You're going to need an easy, comfortable way to carry your baby around with you. This is where a baby carrier comes in. This way, your little one can snuggle in close while you get around to do what you need to do. A good carrier offers your baby secure, safe and comfortable support. In the early days, a baby carrier is the best way to travel with your baby as it promotes intimacy and skin-to-skin contact. If you have a big baby or suffer from back problems, you may find a carrier uncomfortable – in which case you may need to pass on carrier duties to your partner.

9. Baby Bottles with Nipples

You'll need baby bottles whether you're breastfeeding or bottle-feeding. If you're feeding your baby breastmilk, you'll still need a way to feed your baby expressed milk so he or she can be fed without you around. These days, most parents prefer to use glass bottles to avoid the chemicals in plastic passing into the milk.

10. Changing Pad

Most parents designate an area in the room to change their baby's diaper. This changing station is usually made up of a changing pad on a solid, sturdy surface. Keep in mind that you'll be using this station multiple times a day, so it's important that it isn't wobbly, is in an area that gets enough light, and doesn't require mom or dad to crouch over in an uncomfortable position. Some parents also like to have a back-up changing pad in case the main one gets soiled.

11. A Diaper Genie or Pail

You're going to need a proper place to store dirty diapers between trash runs. Regular trash cans don't always do a great job at masking the bad odors – and this is where a diaper genie comes in. A genie or pail is capable of storing a load of dirty diapers without letting the bad smells waft into the room. If you have a big house, a diaper genie may not be absolutely necessary, but if your home is a tighter fit, you're going to want to keep that diaper smell out of the other rooms.

12. Car Seat

You're going to need a car seat as soon as you get into the car with your baby to head home from the hospital. For a newborn baby, it is advised that you purchase a rear-facing car seat. Until the age of two years-old, your baby should *not* use a forward-facing car seat.

13. Stroller

While a baby carrier pretty much always suffices for taking your baby wherever you need to go, you're eventually going to crave the freedom of a stroller – especially for taking your baby outdoors. And once your baby starts getting heavy, a stroller becomes an absolute must-have. Unlike a carrier, a stroller allows a baby to lay flat on his or her back and sleep comfortably. And once your baby ages, they can easily interact with the world while remaining comfortable. One of the other great things about a stroller is that it also gives mom a place to store baby essentials while on-the-go.

14. A Baby Bathtub

Many mothers survive just fine without a baby bathtub, but they make things a lot more convenient when bathing your baby. These days, baby bathtubs come with all kinds of hi-tech features, including temperature indicators. Feel free to purchase whatever makes the most sense for your budget. The most essential feature is the space it provides for your newborn to get wet, but not too submerged. Moms who opt out of the baby bathtub choose to just get in the big bathtub with their newborn in their lap. Or another alternative, using the sink. If you don't have a lot of space in your home, these two alternatives may be the best choice. Whatever you do – baby bathtub or not – do not get a bathtub ring as these pose more dangers than they prevent.

15. A Nursing Bra

When your milk comes in, your breasts are going to get much bigger. This means none of your current bras are going to be very helpful – including your pregnancy bras. To ensure you get the most comfort and support for your breasts, get fitted for a nursing bra. Ideally, you should do this as close to your expected due date as possible and no earlier than a month before. You are unlikely to be in the mood after your baby comes, so doing this beforehand is best.

For Breastfeeding

16. A Breast Pump

If you plan on breastfeeding, a breast pump is a core necessity. This allows you to express and store milk in advance so your baby can be fed even if you're asleep or away. If you find yourself engorged or with an oversupply of milk, a breast pump will be your best friend.

17. Containers or Bags for Milk Storage

After expressing milk, you're going to need a place to store it until it's needed. Ideally, it should be in something that is designed to store breast milk. There are many options for this and it all comes down to personal preference. Moms can take their pick of glass containers, breast milk trays, storage bags, or plastic milk bottles.

18. Nipple Cream or Lanolin Ointment

Believe me, your nipples are going to get sore. While there's no sure way to prevent it entirely if you're breastfeeding, you can take measures to avoid cracked and dry nipples. Applying cream or ointment to your nipples everyday can work wonders.

19. Breast Pads

When breastfeeding a baby, it isn't uncommon for the other breast (the one that's not feeding your baby) to also let out milk. As you'd expect, this can lead to a little and sometimes a lot of leaking. Some moms naturally leak more than others and it may have to do with their supply. Even when you're not breastfeeding, you'll likely experience leaking, especially once your baby starts sleeping longer hours and your body hasn't adjusted to the new schedule. And this is where breast or nursing pads come in to save the day. They prevent milk from leaking through your clothes. Mothers that don't intend to breastfeed also find breast pads helpful sometimes, as it's possible to experience some leaking before milk production dries up.

For Formula Feeding:

20. Formula

This one is a given! If you plan on formula-feeding your baby, make sure you have a large stock of all the formula you need for the next few to several weeks. It's important that the formula you buy is suitable for your newborn. The three types of formula are ready-to-use, powdered, or concentrated liquid. Talk to your doctor to determine the right kind of formula for your baby.

For Postpartum Healing

21. Maxi Pads

If you're planning on a vaginal birth, stock up on some maxi pads. You're going to be bleeding a lot after giving birth; make sure you're underwear and clothing are fully protected with these new mom essentials. You'll be using these for several weeks after giving birth and believe me, tampons will not do. If you're a waste-conscious person and you'd prefer to not use disposable products, know that there are plenty of reusable cloth maxi pads as well. Many moms find these even more comfortable than disposable pads.

22. A Tummy Splint

After pregnancy, many women experience abdominal separation. This is when the left and right stomach muscles separate slightly, resulting in tummy fat that looks disjointed from the rest of the stomach. This isn't just an aesthetic concern, it can also cause constipation, lower back pain, and at its most extreme, a hernia.

Abdominal separation is very common and happens to about two-thirds of pregnant women. Unfortunately, sit-ups can make the issue worse and while time can heal most of the problem, many moms are still left with a little pooch. The tummy splint is the easiest and safest way to minimize the problem after birth. This compression wrap applies light pressure so that mom's body has support and just the right amount of 'push' inwards. Even if abdominal separation isn't a huge concern for you, many moms find a compression wrap very comforting.

How to Start Creating a Birth Plan

On the day of your child's birth, you're probably not going to feel like making any big decisions. This is where the birth plan comes in. Having a birth plan prepared means your decisions and wishes about your baby's delivery are documented ahead of time. When your baby comes knocking, this means all your preferences are clearly outlined – so you can just focus on birthing your little bundle.

Keep in mind that sometimes unpredictable circumstances strike during birth, so there's always a possibility doctors will insist on a different course of action. And you, yourself, may want to make these changes. In any case, it is always helpful to create a birth plan. This step is completely optional, but many moms like having the chance to discuss and think through these decisions ahead of time. This is what you should include in your birth plan:

- **List the basics**

These include your name, contact information, and your doctor's name. If you know which hospital you'll be delivering at, include the name of this hospital too.

- **Name all attendants**

Who of your friends and family would you like to be present in the delivery room? Having this in your birth plan will ensure they're all allowed in during your big moment.

- **Atmosphere preferences**

Think of the environment that you'd most like to give birth in. What do you find calming or soothing? Would you like the lights dimmed or any type of music playing in the background? Are there any items from home that you need beside you to give you strength?

- **Your labor preferences**

Would you like to be photographed or filmed? Would you like to walk around freely? Birthing equipment may be available, such as a birthing stool or chair; include whether you would like anything like this. If you like the idea of being in a tub for labor and delivery, include this in your plan as well. And if you'd prefer to opt out of an episiotomy (snipping of the perineum for easier delivery), say so and be prepared to discuss this with your doctor.

- **Pain management preferences**

When the intensity of labor sets in, what are your preferences around the use of an epidural? What about other pain medications? If you're fine with the use of an epidural or other pain relief, would you like it as soon as possible or would you like to wait and see if you can do without it first? If you don't want any of the above pain medications, are there any alternatives you'd prefer?

- **Delivery preferences**

Would you like the opportunity to watch your baby emerge with a mirror? Many mothers even want to touch their baby's head as it crowns. If you have preferences around whether to have an episiotomy when necessary or to allow natural tearing, mention this. When your baby is out, would you like the father to cut the umbilical cord? If you're having a C-section, would you like the drape removed so you can watch your baby being lifted out of you? Do you want everyone else in the room to be silent so that your voice is the first thing your baby hears? It's possible that you may also have an IV or catheter inserted, so if you want to steer clear of this, include this.

For clarity's sake, it's always best if the birth plan is less than a page long and easy to read. Once you're done, share your birth plan with your partner and your doctor. Their input may be helpful before the plan is finalized.

Chapter 6 - Childbirth & Labor

At last, the time has come! The big day has arrived and everything you've prepared for in your childbirth class stands before you. Hopefully, your hospital bag is fully packed by now – if it isn't, get your partner or family member to gather what you'll need most (pillows, hair ties, and snacks!) and accept they may need to come back later. If it's your first birth, you're likely having it at the hospital either via planned or unplanned C-section, or natural birth. If you have a doula and she's not yet with you, it's time to let her know that your time is finally here.

By now, you, your partner, your doctor, and your doula (if you have one) should be well aware of the decisions laid out in your birth plan. Everyone will be trying their best to honor your wishes, but stay flexible. Unexpected things can happen which makes it difficult to honor very specific preferences; just know that whatever course of action is made, it will be in the best interest of you and your baby.

When it comes to childbirth, a good rule of thumb is to always expect the unexpected. No two births are exactly the same, even from the same mother. This said, there are many things to keep in mind on this big day. It's possible that not all of it will apply to you, but it's always helpful to prepare for the unexpected the best you can.

10 Less-Known Things You Should Know About Vaginal Childbirth & Labor

Everyone knows vaginal childbirth is challenging and painful, but what else? So much happens during labor – stuff you'd never know about unless you'd gone through it! – and all pregnant women should have the complete picture.

1. **Your doctor may not be with you until the very end, and sometimes, not even then.** Despite your many doctor visits, he or she won't really be needed until delivery takes place. Since midwives and other professionals are fully equipped and skilled to handle labor, there's no need for the doctor during this part of the process. The doctor may slip in and out to check in on you, but do not expect more attention than that. It's also possible that your doctor won't even deliver your baby, especially if he or she has partners at the facility.

2. **It's possible you'll get sent home, even if your contractions are real labor contractions.** Even though contractions definitely signify that you're in labor, the reality is that labor can last days. Unless your contractions are very frequent, coming every five minutes or less, then there's a possibility you'll get turned away at the hospital and told to come back later.

3. **The pain might be far more tolerable than you think - or far worse.** There's absolutely no way to predict how painful your childbirth will be. Of course, all women should expect some pain, but I've known many women who were blessed with relatively easy labors and a baby out in under ten minutes. On the other hand, I've also known women who claimed childbirth was even worse than they thought. There's no sure way to know.

4. **You will probably poop in the middle of childbirth.** Many women are horrified to learn this fact, but unfortunately there's no way to ensure it doesn't happen. The reason behind this is simple: when you push out your baby, you engage the same muscles you use to have a bowel movement. In addition to this, your baby creates a lot of pressure on the rectum and colon as it squeezes through the birth canal. It's absolutely essential that

women do not become consumed by self-consciousness when this happens. Doctors are completely used to seeing this happen in the delivery room, as it happens to most women. What doctors do mind is that this self-consciousness can often prevent women from pushing properly, making everyone's job a lot more difficult. Just focus on delivering your baby and know there's no reason to worry about anything else.

5. **There's a possibility you'll throw up or be nauseous.** Not all moms experience this, but many do and it's completely normal. If you're using an epidural, which causes blood pressure to drop, this can bring on nausea or vomiting as it sets in. Though even if you aren't using an epidural, these side effects are still a possibility. While you're giving birth, many of your body's functions slow down or stop, including digestion. And if you have a lot of food in your stomach, it may need to come back up. If you'd like to minimize your risk of vomiting, stop eating and stick to water once you're in active labor. And in early labor, try to only eat light food.

6. **A lot of people will be there over the course of your labor and childbirth.** Although this depends heavily on the type of facility you'll be delivering at, for the most part, it takes more than two or three people to deliver a baby. If you're having your baby in a big hospital, expect to see many different faces over the course of labor and childbirth. Not only will you need a nurse or two, but you'll also need a midwife, the doctor, various assistants, and if your hospital is a teaching hospital, then possibly even medical residents. Don't be alarmed when you see more than a few new faces. It's all completely normal and everyone is just there to help.

7. **Your doctor may need to open you up wider.** To help get your baby out, your doctor may think it is necessary to give

you an episiotomy. This is when an incision is made along your perineum (the skin between your vagina and anus) so your baby can be delivered easier. Doctors usually do this for a good reason but in many cases, it is possible to opt out of it. Speak to your doctor about this beforehand, if you'd like to avoid an episiotomy. But also know that you may want one – it can move things along when you're running out of steam!

8. **You'll deliver far more than just a baby.** Don't worry, this isn't as scary as this sounds. After giving birth, mom is going to need to expel a few things that she no longer needs in her body, namely the placenta (also known as the afterbirth) and lots of blood and tissue. New moms are always alarmed by how much blood comes out of their body after birth; expect it and don't be nervous.

9. **Overwhelming happiness may not be your first emotion after giving birth.** After a physically and emotionally exhausting birth, and labor which may have lasted hours or days, it's normal for mom to be emotionally shut down. This is a normal response while extremely exhausted and it's important that everyone lets mom rest. And mom, too, should not be ashamed that she isn't jumping for joy after such a physically draining experience. Just give mom some time to recharge and she'll wake up with the incredible joy that everyone else is feeling as well.

10. **Childbirth is difficult on partners too.** Of course, it won't be nearly as much of a challenge as it is for mom – but that doesn't mean it isn't a challenge for dad or other birth partners! It isn't uncommon for nurses to take someone out of the delivery room because it's too upsetting to watch their loved one in so much pain. If this happens, do not fault your partner for having this reaction. Many partners do.

4 Things to Do for a Safer C-Section

There's no need to worry about your C-section. It's true that it comes with more risks than a vaginal birth, but this is true of all surgeries. Complications from cesareans are rare and women generally have a lot of control when it comes to avoiding these complications. Many new mothers are interested in the precautions they can take before and after their C-section. Here's what you can do to ensure you steer clear of the risks of a C-section.

1. **Wash yourself with antibacterial soap before surgery.** Doing this ensures that there is less bacteria in the area where you will be cut, therefore reducing your risk for infection – one of the biggest risks associated with C-sections.

2. **Do not shave your pubic hair yourself before surgery.** If it needs to be removed, it will be trimmed carefully by surgical staff. Shaving can increase your risk of infection.

3. **Keep warm the best you can.** Getting cold before or during a C-section can raise your risk of infection very slightly. Make sure you're snug and warm in all the blankets you need.

4. **Walk as soon as you can after surgery.** Yes, you will be sore, but walking shortly after surgery gets your blood moving again – and this is essential for reducing the risk of blood clots. Whatever you do, don't overdo physical activity. Just make sure you get some time on your feet to start the healing process.

The Lowdown on Epidural Anesthesia

When it comes to pain relief during childbirth, epidural anesthesia is the most prominently used. Not only is it administered for c-sections and vaginal deliveries, but it also relieves pain for a number of other surgeries and body pain from a prolapsed disc.

How is an Epidural Administered?

The epidural is injected with a needle into the lower back, specifically in the area around the spinal nerves. A local anesthesia is given in this same area prior to the epidural, so mothers do not feel too much pain from the second round of anesthetic. Epidurals numb the body below the place of injection, so mom's birthing pains are lessened significantly and yet she can still stay awake during childbirth or c-section. It takes roughly 15-20 minutes for the anesthetic to take effect. Since the bottom half of the body is numb, a catheter is usually inserted until the effects of the epidural wear off.

Why Should You Get an Epidural?

An epidural is completely optional for vaginal births. Many women claim they absolutely need it and others cope just fine without one. The biggest and most obvious advantage to the epidural is, of course, having a far more painless or, in some cases, *completely* painless delivery. Many women find the pain of childbirth unbearable and if labor was difficult as well, some mothers just can't handle anymore. Free of pain, many mothers find that they are completely clear-headed during labor.

Why Shouldn't You Get an Epidural?

There are a few reasons why some moms opt out of the epidural. Some women do not like the sound of the side effects, which can include headaches, nausea, urination during delivery and inability to control it for a short while afterwards, temporary nerve damage, and difficulty walking. Due to the lack of sensation in the lower half of the body, women under epidural anesthesia tend to also have a hard time pushing effectively during delivery. So even though birth becomes painless, an epidural can prolong the overall time of labor. After birth, the anesthetic still needs time to wear off, so mom won't be able to feel her legs for a short time after.

Like with most things, epidurals come with their own risks. There is always a small possibility (roughly 0.5%) that moms will develop a post-dural puncture headache – a severe headache that sets in anywhere from a day to a week after an epidural. The pain from this headache will become intense when upright in a seated or standing position but lessen when lying down. Accompanying the pain, there may also be nausea, vomiting, neck pain and an extreme sensitivity to light. Despite being painful, this is easily treated by a doctor.

Will an Epidural Affect the Baby?

Unfortunately, a lot more studies need to be done on this subject. There is some evidence to show that epidurals have a subtle effect on newborns, but this hasn't been explored in detail. What we do know is that epidurals do not harm a baby, as far as we know, and if there are any side effects, they are not serious. For example, some studies have shown that epidurals may lead to issues breastfeeding, namely with getting the baby to "latch on" to the breast – but this does no lasting damage to the baby.

7 Helpful Tricks for Pushing that Baby Out

1. **Push as if you're going to the bathroom, i.e. having a bowel movement.** This always throws first-time moms off! Naturally, they think that if they're trying to push a baby out and *not* go to the bathroom, they shouldn't be using those muscles. This is wrong! And this is why it's difficult to avoid having a bowel movement while giving birth. If it feels as if you're pooping, you're on the right track! Don't be embarrassed and just get it done.

2. **Use big focused pushes instead of smaller frantic ones.** Many first-time pushers try to conserve their energy and opt for light but frequent pushes. These will prove very ineffective and may just prolong the time spent in labor. Put focus and a

lot of energy into every push! Frequent and intense pushes are far better than prolonged pushes.

3. **Don't strain or push with your upper body.** This won't impact your baby's birth but it may leave mom with facial bruising or bloodshot eyes. When mothers let out an intense push, they instinctively pull their upper body into it as well. To avoid bruising in the upper body, push only with your lower body and do not strain your face too hard.

4. **Don't be afraid to try a different position.** Most women give birth lying on their back but other positions have proven much more helpful for getting a baby out. If lying on your back isn't doing the trick, try squatting upright. This way, gravity can assist with birthing your baby.

5. **Keep breathing and do not hold your breath for longer than a few seconds.** When in intense pain, many people naturally start to hold their breath. Resist doing this when you're giving birth. Take deep breaths whenever you can and especially before each big push.

6. **Don't push until you feel like pushing.** Being in labor doesn't mean you're ready to push. You'll know when you are! And when the time comes...

7. **Push when you feel like pushing!** Your body knows when the right time is. In fact, pushing is more like an involuntary response and reflex. You'll have to try hard to not do it. If you know you're fully dilated and the urge comes, go for it.

The Best Positions for Pushing with an Epidural

Epidurals will make the pain of childbirth a lot more manageable. In some cases, it may eliminate the pain entirely.

Unfortunately, along with the elimination of pain, an epidural can also numb or diminish urges to push. These urges are very helpful when it comes to getting a baby out as they basically tell mom when she should be pushing. When mom can't tell what's happening with her body, pushing the baby out becomes a lot more complicated. Thankfully, there are many birthing positions that may make it easier on mom and baby. If you're taking an epidural, keep these positions in mind:

- Lying on the side.
- Kneeling by or at the foot of the bed while leaning over.
- Squatting with support from others.
- Lying on the back with legs in stirrups or supports.
- Upright sitting position.
- Half-sitting with knees pulled towards you.

7 Little-Known Things about C-Sections

1. **You'll still feel your baby coming out.** It won't be painful in any way but you'll still be able to feel a vague tugging at your abdomen. If you've had other types of surgery before, it is not too different from that.

2. **The surgical team may seem unusually casual.** Even though this is your first birth, the surgical staff taking care of you have done this plenty of times before. Many first time moms are taken aback by the casual and laid-back chatter amongst the staff. Learn to see this as a positive thing! It means everything is going exactly as planned so you can just relax.

3. **If you want to watch your baby come out, you can.** Even if you haven't included this preference in your birth plan, you can

still ask to have this arrangement on the day. Just make sure you're ready to see a lot of blood!

4. **Your partner may not be prepared to see you cut open.** It's customary for doctors to warn birth partners about what they might see – and most will advise just focusing on your face – but squeamish or not, partners sometimes can't resist the temptation to look. It's not the easiest sight to behold so be prepared to see your partner get a little pale!

5. **Doctors might strap you down.** This doesn't always happen but it isn't uncommon. Many mothers find this unusual but it's all to ensure the utmost safety. The last thing anyone wants is movement that makes surgery more difficult. The good news is you'll barely feel your arms and they may even unstrap you once your baby is out.

6. **The birth will be quick but the stitching up will take some time.** In fact, your baby will be out within the first ten minutes of the surgery starting. Stitching you up, however, can take up to 45 minutes. This said, many moms barely notice the time going by when they're getting sewn up. Why? Because they're just thrilled the baby is out!

7. **You'll be numb for quite some time.** Thanks to the pain medication, you won't feel it at all the first time you touch your C-section scar. It's also possible you won't feel a thing the first time your baby breastfeeds. This upsets some moms but there's no reason to be – trust me, you'll feel your baby breastfeeding *a lot* after this point. The most important thing is that you and your baby are healthy, and a long, beautiful journey lays ahead of you.

Chapter 7 - Postpartum Care

First-time mom, you are a pillar of strength. You've finally brought your baby into the world and now, no one underestimates the fortitude you clearly possess. The journey only continues. After the difficulties of pregnancy and childbirth, it's absolutely crucial that you get in the habit of taking care of yourself, as well as your baby. Being the strong mother you are, it'll come naturally to you to just power through no matter how you're feeling. While this is an admirable ability, this attitude shouldn't dictate your lifestyle from now on. Not only are you transitioning into a new big role, but your body is also healing.

To ensure you take care of yourself in the best way possible, here are some of the many things you can do to nourish your inner and outer well-being. Get used to listening to your body so you can better identify what you need at any given moment.

What Every Mother Needs to Do after Giving Birth

1. Get A Lot of Rest

Needless to say, mom is going to need to rest and recharge. This can be difficult when you have a newborn. You'll find that your baby wakes up every few hours, needing to be fed, so getting a solid 7-8 hours will be pretty much impossible. A good rule of thumb is to sleep whenever your baby sleeps. Even if sleep only lasts for an hour or two at a time, these hours add up and can really help.

2. Get Help from Loved Ones

Whether it's your partner, family, friends or all of the above, make sure you get all the help you need with household chores and other responsibilities. Ideally, everything in the home should be taken care of, leaving you to focus on feeding the baby and taking care of yourself, until you've had more time to recover.

3. Get Good Nutrition

So many nursing others end up neglecting their diet and nutrition because they are just so tired. This is where your loved ones come in. Get a family member or your partner to help you adhere to a healthy diet; this will aid you greatly on the road to recovery. According to lactation experts, it's best if mom eats whenever she is hungry – but ideally, she should be eating an overall balanced diet with the right amount of calories and fat. These include:

- Whole grains, such as whole wheat or oatmeal.

- Unpasteurized dairy products, such as milk or yogurt. If possible, stick to low-fat or fat-free options.

- Fruits in any form, including 100% fruit juice. Tired moms may find that juice or a smoothie is the best and easiest way to get their fill of fruit.

- Vegetables – ideally a variety of them, including leafy greens, legumes, orange, red, and starchy vegetables.

- Protein with less of an emphasis on meats, especially red meats. The best proteins for recovering new moms are beans, seeds, nuts, and fish. For other types of meat, make sure you're only consuming lean meat.

9 Completely Normal Long-Term & Short-Term Effects of Pregnancy and Childbirth

1. Hair Loss

Remember when pregnancy hormones gave you thick, lush hair? A drop in those hormones means you're going to experience the opposite. After giving birth, many moms go through a period of hair loss. But don't worry, this isn't forever. This shouldn't last for more than five months.

2. Hemorrhoids

There's going to be general soreness in your nether regions after birth; if you notice some of this pain coming from your anus, then there's a good chance that you have hemorrhoids. This swelling can make bowel movements even more difficult than they already are with an episiotomy wound or tearing. If your doctor hasn't already given you a stool softener, it's time to ask for one. If you'd like other forms of treatment, try an over-the-counter cream for hemorrhoids or wear pads that contain a numbing solution. Hemorrhoids are easily treated, so there's no need to fret about this one.

3. Incontinence

I warned you about this, didn't I? Pregnancy and childbirth can really pull a number on your pelvic floor muscles. When the muscles that control urination, bowel movements, and passing gas are stretched or injured, it can lead to some frustrating side effects. Most moms experience some level of stress incontinence, which is when a little urine leaks out while laughing, coughing, or sneezing. Incontinence tends to improve after a few weeks but it isn't uncommon to have some lasting effects. Hopefully, you've been practicing your pelvic floor exercises! If you haven't, try doing them now.

4. Contractions

While the worst contractions are long behind you, it's normal to experience some cramping after giving birth. These are called afterbirth pains and they'll be the most intense on the few days right after childbirth. These contractions are a natural result of your uterus returning to its regular prepregnancy size. After a few days, you can expect afterbirth pains to gradually fade away.

5. Constipation

In the days that follow childbirth, it is extremely common to have some constipation. This tends to be caused by anesthesia and pain-relieving medication given to you at the hospital. These can slow down the function of your bowels for a short period of time. Some mothers also find themselves constipated out of the fear and anxiety of hurting their perineum. Stay fully hydrated and eat fiber-rich foods to ease constipation. If you think it might be anxiety causing this problem, talk to your doctor about using a stool softener. Constipation generally isn't a real problem unless you've gone four days after birth without having a bowel movement. At that point, contact your doctor anyway.

6. Wider Hips

Many women discover their body shape has changed after giving birth. Namely, their hips seem slightly wider. While some of this is down to pregnancy weight gain that will subside after a few months, it isn't uncommon for a woman's shape to see some permanent changes. During pregnancy, a woman's pelvis bone structure changes to allow a baby to move smoothly through the birth canal. Not every woman will find that this change lingers on, but a significant number do.

7. Mood Changes

I'll say this now and remind you later: don't feel guilty about your mood swings! Many moms are under the mistaken impression that they'll pop out a baby and have impermeable joy. This is a total myth and it leads to a lot of needless shame for a mom that just needs a break. Yes, you'll feel happy but you'll also go through a rollercoaster of other emotions. It's a combination of hormones and the fact you're just exhausted after the last nine months. Don't be hard on yourself! We'll get more in-depth with this later on.

8. Lower Sex Drive

For the same reason the mood swings come, a lower sex drive is very common in postpregnancy. This is especially true for breastfeeding women whose estrogen levels plummet even more from feeding their baby. Most women claim it takes, on average, a year for their sex drive to return to its normal state. But some only feel these effects for a few months. These effects will vary from woman to woman, as with most changes.

9. Melasma

If you've noticed darkened patches of skin on your cheeks, forehead, and/or upper lip, then you have melasma – and you're not alone. Melasma is triggered by any change in hormones. 50-70% of pregnant women are affected by it and many find it lingers long after they give birth. Most signs of melasma fade after a year but you may find that some dark spots need further treatment. Before you seek out the high-strength skincare that is usually prescribed for melasma, wait until you're no longer breastfeeding your baby.

10. Darker Skin on the Areolas & Labia

As I mentioned in a previous chapter, a woman's areolas get darker and sometimes bigger during pregnancy. Some women find that their nipples and areolas remain this darker shade even after giving birth. This isn't the only thing that changes, however; the labia, too, can become a darker shade and you may even see this same darkening with moles.

How to Help the Body Heal from Birth

Every mother is sore and in pain after childbirth. Depending on the type of birth you had, you're likely aching in more places than one. C-section or vaginal birth, doctors recommend that you abstain from sex for a few to several weeks. Absolutely do not try to do it anyway or your body will pay the price.

Follow your doctor's instructions and there will be nothing to worry about. You're most definitely on the road to recovery already, but here are a few other things that you can do to speed up the healing process.

Caring for Your C-Section Scar

Your doctor or nurse should have given you some helpful instructions about how to care for your C-section scar. It all comes down to two things: clean and dry. Ideally, you should be cleaning it gently every day with a little bit of mild soap and water. After washing, pat the scar dry with a clean towel. Most doctors will tell you it is completely fine to apply some petroleum jelly or an antibiotic ointment to your scar. However, some doctors feel it's best to let it be after washing and drying, with no oil or ointment whatsoever. None of these practices will do harm to your scar so feel free to choose what feels right for you, or ask your doctor what his or her preferred approach is.

Whenever you can, let your scar air out; air can help skin injuries heal faster. In addition to this, try to wear loose clothing to avoid rubbing against your scar. Your doctor should have also mentioned this, but avoid all exercise, especially during the first several weeks.

If your scar shows signs of swelling or redness in the skin surrounding it, or starts oozing out any liquid, make sure to contact your doctor as soon as possible.

Caring for Your Perineum

The perineum tends to be one of the most sore areas after giving birth. Whether you had it cut during delivery or it tore naturally, you're likely eager for some relief. Using an ice pack on the area every few hours can work wonders – especially the day after giving birth. After urinating, take extra care to gently clean the area, as urine can irritate the cut or torn skin. Spray or lightly splash some warm water on the perineum to prevent irritation. Do this before and after urinating.

Improving Urinary or Fecal Incontinence

Hopefully, you've been doing the pelvic floor exercises in Chapter Three! These will have given you some strength against incontinence. If you weren't quite so diligent about it, that's okay! You can start doing them as soon as you feel you are well enough. These would take effect immediately, but if you stick with it, you'll see improvements soon enough.

Easing Painful or Sore Breasts

Aside from using lanolin ointment on your nipples, make sure to also let your breasts breathe after each feeding session. Being exposed to cool air can have a soothing effect on the skin. Some mothers find that using a warm compress or heating pad on sore breasts can really help a lot.

Soothing General Achiness 'Down There'

If the pain gets too uncomfortable, the use of painkillers is always an option, especially acetaminophen can help greatly with pain in the perineum. Other soothing methods include taking a sitz bath and using a heating pad. Many mothers also swear by witch hazel pads, which can be used in conjunction with an ice pack to ease pain in the vagina and/or postpartum hemorrhoids.

Everything You Need to Know About Postpartum Depression

The birth of a baby brings incredible joy into the lives of two lucky parents. It is entirely common, however, to feel a range of other emotions. With joy, there may also be fear and anxiety about being a good enough carer or parent. And mothers may even feel the 'baby blues' starting as soon as a couple of days after delivery. These feelings are very normal and for many mothers, the blues can disappear in just a couple of weeks. When the baby blues last for an extended period of time, however, this is called postpartum depression. The symptoms of postpartum depression include:

- A pervasive feeling that you can't bond with your baby.
- Complete depletion of energy.
- Insomnia or oversleeping.
- Loss of appetite or overeating.
- Withdrawal from close friends and family.
- Excessive crying spells.
- Strong feelings of being an inadequate or bad mother.
- Restlessness and anxiety.
- Mood swings or general depression.
- Guilt, shame, and feelings of worthlessness.

If these symptoms persist for over two weeks, it is essential that new mothers seek out help for postpartum depression. This is especially important if symptoms cross the line into postpartum psychosis, marked most notably by feelings of confusion, delusions or hallucinations, obsessive thoughts that revolve around the baby, paranoia, and perhaps even thoughts or attempts to hurt oneself or the baby. The longer these conditions are left untreated, the longer they will continue. Help from a medical professional can allow new mothers to get back to a healthy frame of mind so they can enjoy their new role, as they deserve.

9 Soul-Soothing Self-Care Ideas for a First-Time Mom

1. Invite a Friend Over

If you're feeling up to it, why not invite a friend over? Once your newborn is a little more settled in and you've had time to recharge, getting some time with a friend whose company you love can be incredibly healing. While your baby is napping, you could have lunch together in your home and enjoy a movie or TV show. This is also a great time to make new friends with other first time moms. If you know anyone else who just had a baby, this may be the perfect time to form a bond.

2. Enjoy a Warm or Hot Bath

This self-care method isn't just soul-soothing, but it's also body-soothing, especially for sensitive areas that are sore. Feel free to also dim the lights, play music in the background, or light candles if you'd find it more comforting. You can do this at all hours of the day, whenever you need it the most. Do it between your baby's naps or simply ask your partner to take over for a while. Since you're probably tired, just make sure you don't fall asleep in the tub!

3. Pamper Yourself with a Massage or Manicure

You deserve to pamper yourself, new mom! Many new mothers feel guilty when they take time away from their baby to get pampered

– but this guilt needs to stop. As long as you're not doing this excessively, you're giving yourself exactly what you need to be the best mom for your baby. Your body has gone through *a lot*; let yourself sit back so you can be taken care of for a moment. Whether it's a massage, a manicure, or a pedicure, do something that allows you to be still and be soothed.

4. Write in a Journal

Many new mothers love taking up journal-writing after they've had a baby. Even those who have never had a journal before. Documenting these early days can be very special and some moms even do it with the intention of sharing the journal with their child once they are old enough. Writing can center the soul and allow us to sit, breathe, and observe our everyday lives. If it feels like everything is changing and you haven't had time to yourself, the act of writing and recording can feel very anchoring. Deciding to not share this journal with anyone is fine too. Allow yourself to just feel what you're feeling and give yourself a safe space in a private journal. Find a time each day or every other day to write an entry in your journal, perhaps during one of your newborn's morning naps.

5. Reconnect with your Partner

With a new baby in the mix, many couples become overwhelmed and forget to take time to themselves. I don't just mean sitting down to watch TV in silence, but to actually talk and discuss how they're doing with the new changes in their lives. Remember what you did before the baby came along. Talk about what you used to talk about, make light of funny scenarios, and laugh together. Foster and nurture your connection, and you'll both find yourselves soul-soothed.

6. Dive Back Into an Old Hobby or Interest – or Find New Ones!

You may have a new baby but that doesn't mean you have to discard your hobbies and interests. In fact, it may be emotionally and mentally beneficial for you to get back into them. Studies have shown that when we regularly do something that takes us away from our usual train of thought, it triggers anti-oxidation in our body and combats stress. If you enjoy knitting, get back into it during the times you have to yourself. If you'd like to start sketching or blogging, now's not too late to start. Take your mind away, momentarily, and let your body destress.

7. Treat Yourself to Fun Soap, Lotion & Other Body Care

Now's the time to indulge in body care goodness. Whether it's LUSH, Bath & Body Works, or something else, treat yourself to products that make your body and skin feel amazing. The time you get to yourself in the shower counts as self-care; get all the fun flavors or flavors you can find and let yourself be soothed. If you have a C-section scar or any kind of stitching or tearing on your perineum, make sure to not rub any of these products directly on these areas.

8. Go on Frequent Walks

Walking is a great way for a new mother to get some exercise. It's safe for her recovering body, allows her to get some fresh air, and it can also improve her mood. Practice this healthy habit any way that works for you. You could take your baby out in his or her stroller, or you could ask your partner to watch your little one while you get some time alone to destress with a leisurely stroll. It may seem like too simple an act to make a difference, but you'll be surprised by how clear-headed and relaxed you can be from a walk. The best part is it doesn't have to take long and you can do it almost anywhere. Bring some music and headphones for an even more relaxing walk.

9. Take Care of the Basics

Sometimes the best self-care just requires doing the basics and doing them well. Many overwhelmed new moms are so exhausted they forget to do this. Eat nourishing food that you love, drink lots of water, use a lovely scented soap in the shower, and get some rest during your baby's naps. If you're not up for socializing, free yourself from those responsibilities. Just focus on taking care of yourself in the most basic but essential ways.

Chapter 8 - Your Newborn Baby

Holding your first baby in your arms is an unparalleled experience. To think you created this new life with your own body! What utter magic. You're going to have a marvelous time getting to know this tiny little human, but as you'll quickly realize, it's not all tickles and cuddles. Tiny humans need a lot of care and comfort. Since they don't have mom's strength yet, they're still very delicate and vulnerable. This chapter is packed with information on how to properly care for a newborn baby. As your baby gets older, your techniques and strategies will evolve as well – but for now, keep a close eye on these crucial details.

11 Things You Should Know About Newborn Babies

1. **It's normal for their skin to be dry.** After all, they were submerged in a wet womb before promptly hitting the air. The dryness can sometimes be alarming to new moms and dads, but it's actually completely harmless and there's nothing you need to do about it.

2. **If your newborn is fussy, try to mimic the conditions of the womb.** Consider how it felt for the baby to be snug inside your body and try to recreate that same environment. Try swaddling or gentle swinging, and accompany this by a light whooshing or shushing noise. You may even find that a warm bath has a soothing effect on your newborn.

3. **Make sponge baths the norm for the first couple of weeks** – or specifically, until the umbilical cord falls off. A sponge bath makes it easier to keep the umbilical cord dry, which is what it needs to fall off quickly.

4. **Expect some bleeding when the umbilical cord falls off.** Just think of it as a scab peeling off. Blood is normal and it's no reason to be alarmed.

5. **Newborns are near-sighted.** Just after birth, a newborn baby can only see about 8 to 12 inches in front of their faces. Everything beyond that is blurry and cannot be distinguished. As the months pass, your baby's sight will gradually get stronger. At three months old, shapes and colors will be much clearer.

6. **Don't fret if your baby loses a bit of weight.** A few days after giving birth, it isn't uncommon for babies to lose about five to ten percent of their body weight. This is not a sign that your baby is underfed. In fact, you'll discover your baby has gained more weight after a couple of weeks past birth.

7. **Breastfed babies have less smelly poop.** A strange fact but it's true! Just after birth, all babies have the same type of poop. But once you establish a feeding routine and decide on how you'll find your baby, the nature of their poop will quickly change. What does it depend on? Whether they're formula-fed or breastfed. Remarkably, the poop of breastfed babies does not stink at all.

8. **It's normal for newborns to have birthmarks.** These will appear pink or peach-colored on their face or neck. Some parents are even surprised to see these marks get more red when they're in distress. Roughly a third of babies will have these marks, so it's usually no cause for concern. But if you notice skin discoloration or strange bumps, it's always best to speak to a doctor. Otherwise, these harmless pink marks tend to disappear within six months.

9. **Newborns can leak milk.** In fact, you may even notice that some newborns appear to have tiny raised breasts. This and any milk leakage is completely normal, and will not last beyond a few weeks. The reason behind this occurrence is that newborns absorb some of mom's estrogen hormones while they're in the womb. In baby daughters, it can also lead to vaginal discharge or mini periods.

10. **Most newborns like facing the right side when they sleep.** And many experts think this may be linked to why most people are right-handed. Only about 15% babies prefer to face the left side when they sleep.

11. **They can remember what you ate while you were pregnant with them.** And most fascinating of all, this may influence their own personal flavor preferences. Everything that mom eats after four months of pregnancy affects the way their amniotic fluid tastes and they'll know instantly when this same flavor comes up again in mom's breastmilk. If mom ate a lot of meals with heavy garlic flavoring, you can bet that baby will be drawn to garlic later on.

6 Must-Know Rules About Formula-Feeding

1. **Do not reuse formula your baby doesn't finish, even if you refrigerate it first.** It becomes a breeding ground for bacteria after a certain time and this is not helped by storing it. If, however, you've prepared formula that your baby never even touches the nipple of, then it's safe to store for 24 hours. Do not do this if your baby has had his or her mouth on the bottle's nipple at all.

2. **Do not use prepared formula that's been left out for more than an hour.** The bacteria that grows beyond this time can make your baby ill.

3. **Store formula in the back of your fridge, which is where it is coldest** – but do *not* freeze formula. Freezing formula negatively affects its texture and consistency. While this isn't dangerous, you baby will be far less likely to drink it this way.

4. **Serve formula as soon as it's prepared and warmed.** As soon as it has time to sit, bacteria starts to accumulate. Give it to your baby before it has time to become a breeding ground.

5. **Be a total clean freak when it comes to your baby's formula.** This is one of the few times it's completely appropriate to go nuts over every detail. Make sure you wash your hands before handling your baby's formula and the counter on which it's being prepared. In addition to this, always clean and then properly dry the lid of your formula. Like I said, be a clean freak!

6. **Do not heat up formula in the microwave.** Doing this will heat the formula up unevenly, making extremely hot spots in the solution which are likely to burn your baby's mouth. The best way to heat up formula is with a bottle warmer. If you don't intend on purchasing one, leave bottled formula to stand in a bowl of hot water for just a few minutes. This should do the trick!

Foods to Limit or Avoid While Breastfeeding

You may not be pregnant anymore, but if you're breastfeeding, your baby will still affected by what you eat and drink. For this reason, you'll need to watch what enters your body. Not everything on this list needs to be completely eliminated from your diet; you'll just need to moderate the amount you eat or do so with precaution. Foods you need to limit will not harm your baby in any way, but they may bring about an undesired reaction or behavior, making it more difficult for mom and dad to establish a healthy dynamic. It is important to note that every baby is different and some 'foods to limit' may be more compatible with your newborn.

Foods to Limit or Moderate

- **Spicy Food**

Hot spices can have an affect on how your milk tastes and interacts with your baby's system. Most babies can handle it, but in large amounts or too much frequency, it may induce, colic, gas, or even diarrhea. Some babies are less tolerant towards spice so always pay close attention to see what your baby can handle.

- **Certain Herbs**

Herbs such as peppermint, sage, thyme, oregano, and parsley should be used sparingly. While they aren't dangerous to the baby in any way, they are well-known to reduce a mother's milk supply. On the other hand, feel free to enjoy them if you're struggling with an oversupply of milk or trying to wean your baby off breast milk.

- **'Gassy Vegetables'**

No mom should flat out avoid gassy vegetables, but in the early days, you may need to watch your baby to see how he or she reacts. Gassy vegetables include onions, broccoli, cabbage, cauliflower, peppers, and garlic; some babies can handle these just fine, but others can get extremely uncomfortable and gassy.

- **Caffeine**

Breastfeeding mothers still have to avoid caffeine, but they can consume about 100g more than they used to. This said, some moms choose to opt out of caffeine since it can give their baby sleep problems and make them very fussy. Remember that caffeine isn't just in coffee, it's also in chocolate, energy drinks, and certain teas.

- **Alcohol**

Doctors still say the safest option is to avoid alcohol, but breastfeeding mothers no longer *have* to. There are very reliable ways to get a drink in without it affecting the baby. Breastfeeding mothers should limit themselves to a small glass of wine or a half-pint of beer a day and absolutely no more than that. As with everything in your diet, alcohol can pass through your breast milk to your baby. It hasn't proven to be harmful in very small amounts, so it's essential that mothers limit how much gets through. They can do so by:

I. Waiting at least three hours after drinking to breastfeed the baby.

II. Drinking while breastfeeding, as it takes about 25 minutes for alcohol to enter breast milk.

III. Feeding the baby from stored breast milk when alcohol is still in mom's system.

It's also important that mothers stick to their alcohol limit per day. The more alcohol is consumed in one sitting, the longer it stays in your system.

Foods to Avoid

This one is simple: avoid all other foods that were in the 'Quit List' in Chapter 1. This means no high-mercury fish or unpasteurized dairy. If you're a seafood lover, make sure tuna, swordfish, mackerel, and shark are off your plate. And if you're a cheese nut, always check if it's pasteurized first.

How to Prevent Sudden Infant Death Syndrome

Sudden Infant Death Syndrome, also known as SIDS or Crib Death, is easily every parent's worst nightmare. It is the name given to the spontaneous death of a sleeping baby under one year-old. What makes SIDS even more harrowing is the fact that experts still aren't sure why it happens and there are no warning signs to watch out for. Unfortunately, there is no sure way to prevent SIDS, but you can take measures to lower your baby's risk. The good news is that these preventative measures seem to work; the SIDS rate has dropped by over 60% since they were made official to the public. Here are the best tips available on how to safeguard against SIDS:

1. **Lay your baby to sleep on a firm and bare mattress.** Even though it may seem as if an adorable little human needs something soft, firm mattresses are actually the best choice for SIDS prevention. Soft and fluffy paddings or quilts actually raise the chance suffocation or smothering. All you need is a firm mattress and a fitted sheet or a simple bassinet. And yes, this does mean *no* soft toys or crim bumpers.

2. **Put your baby to sleep on his or her back.** During the first year, they should never at any point be put to sleep on their side or stomach. If anyone else is taking care of your baby, it's important that you let them know this important detail as well. Many sitters believe that a fussy baby can be calmed if they're left on their stomach; whether or not this is true, the raised risk of SIDS means it is not worth finding out. Don't assume that every child care provider knows this and always let them know.

3. **Breastfeed your baby for as long as possible.** Even if you plan on formula-feeding eventually, see how long you can keep breastfeeding part of your baby's routine. Ideally, you should do this for six months, if you can. Remarkably, experts have found that breastfed babies have up to 50% of a lower risk of getting SIDS. The reasons why aren't very clear but it may be due to the fact that breast milk protects babies from infections, some of which could be responsible for SIDS. All this said, a

breastfeeding mother that drinks alcohol actually raises her child's risk.

4. **Do not let your newborn sleep in the same bed as mom, dad, or another child.** While it's completely fine to cuddle and feed your baby in bed, avoid falling asleep together as this, too, raises the risk of suffocation and smothering. Accidents have occurred where a sleeping parent rolls against or onto their baby, restricting their breathing. Avoid this risk by sleeping in separate beds and not breastfeeding your baby in a position where you may fall asleep.

5. **Keep baby's crib in mom's bedroom.** Studies have shown that a baby who sleeps in mom's bedroom (but not in her bed) has a lower risk of SIDS. For this reason, experts tend to advise that newborns don't sleep in their own room until they're older than six months.

6. **Absolutely do not smoke around your baby.** Secondhand smoke is another major risk factor for SIDS. If a smoker is going to be around your baby, make sure that they do not smoke anywhere near the baby. If it helps, let them know of the risks so that they understand what's at stake.

7. **Make sure your baby doesn't overheat.** As you'd expect, overheating increases a baby's risk of SIDS. When your baby goes to sleep, have him or her dressed in comfortable clothes made of a light material. And as long as the room temperature is comfortable for an adult, then it's perfect for your baby.

8. **Don't give honey to an infant.** In very young children, honey can lead to an illness called botulism. While more research needs to be done on this subject, there is evidence to suggest that botulism is linked to SIDS.

And a final note: there are many products out there that wild claims about being able to lower a baby's SIDS risk – keep in mind that these are *just* wild claims. There is no evidence that any of these products, including electronic respirators and cardiac monitors, are effective or even safe.

It's Bath Time!

Bath time can be an incredibly fun and adorable experience with a newborn; you'll be pleased to know that this ritual only gets cuter as they get older. But when things get wet and slippery, the chance of an accident happening gets even higher. This is why it's very important that parents are prepared and attentive during their child's bath time. Follow these tips to make sure bath time is safe, efficient, and comfortable for your baby.

- **Establish a bathtime routine**

Choose a time of day that works for baby's bath time and try to stick to that routine. It's the best way to start setting your baby's body clock. Many moms prefer an evening bathtime routine since the time spent in water is very relaxing and sometimes makes baby sleepy. Over time, they begin to make the connection between bathtime and sleeptime, understanding that these activities go hand and hand. But this said, it's completely up to you and what works for your lifestyle. Morning bath routines are just as wonderful! And remember that just because you've established a routine doesn't mean you have to follow it religiously; if baby is hungry and bathtime needs to be postponed, that's fine too!

- **Have everything you need closeby**

Think of all the supplies you'll need while washing your baby and for right after, and have them within arm's reach. The last thing you want to do is to gather up your wet newborn mid-bath to rush to a different room. Make it easy on yourself! Have all bath time products and drying essentials ready nearby.

- **Water should be warm but not hot**

Before putting baby in the bath, test the water temperature with your elbow, one of the body's more sensitive areas. The water needs to be comfortably warm – not hot and not cold – around 98-100 °F. In order to get just the right temperature, I advise running the cold water first and the hot water after. Do not put your baby in running water. Being exposed to too-hot water for just a second can be enough to scald baby's skin. If you can, also try to keep the room temperature relatively warm, as naked babies can lose body heat very quickly.

- **Don't leave your baby sitting in water for too long**

Ideally, bath time should be at least five minutes and no longer than ten. When babies are left in water for too long, their skin becomes at risk of drying out, especially since it's already pretty dry. In extreme cases, babies can even catch hypothermia, a condition caused by losing body heat faster than you can produce it. And needless to say, you should also not leave your baby sitting or lying in water unattended. You must always stay present during your baby's bath.

- **Use a mild and baby-friendly soap**

A baby's skin is sensitive; for bath times, only use gentle soaps that are, ideally, free of fragrances. The chemicals and oils that are in mom and dad's soap are likely to irritate their skin – even if the packaging looks inviting! To safeguard against skin irritation, I'd even advise using just a small amount of soap and only using it towards the end of bath time. When a baby sits in soapy water for too long, irritation can also develop that way.

- **Wash baby girls from front to back**

This isn't just a tip for bath time, it is also an important piece of advice for diaper-changing. Whether you're wiping or washing a baby girl, you should always go from front to back. This is to avoid anything harmful from getting into her most sensitive area. To be extra safe, you should also steer clear of using soap on her vagina, as oftentimes this can lead to skin irritation.

- **Do not put newborns in a bath seat or ring**

In fact, all babies under one year-old should not be in a bath seat. The reason is simple: these babies are just too small for a bath seat. Too-little babies can easily slide out of the seat since they aren't yet able to fully support themselves. And on top of this, bath seats can easily collapse, potentially leading to the submersion of a baby's face in water. It's also possible for babies to get stuck in or under these unwieldy contraptions. At this point in your child's life, the support of mom or dad's arms are more than enough to keep them safe and comfortable. Sometimes 'simple' really is better.

By now, I don't need to tell you that raising a newborn is hard work. There's a lot of information out there about how to do it right – at the end of the day, what matters most of all is what's safest for your baby.

Enjoy these precious moments with your newborn baby. If there's anything that has struck me about having a newborn baby, it's this: time goes by so fast! In fact, the newborn stage doesn't seem to last long at all. Before you know it, you have a toddler and then a smart-mouthed kid (or at least I do!), and you're left wondering, "Where did all that time go?"

So, as stressed-out and exhausted as you are, take the time to snap a mental picture of these early days. You'll cherish these memories forever.

First-Time Mom

Conclusion

Congratulations on making it to the end of *First Time Mom*! One of the best things you can do as a new parent is to stay informed; that's what you've done by finishing this book! You are leaps and strides closer to being the best parent you can be for your little one. Many new moms feel overwhelmed by how much information there is to read and remember. Just know that your immediate concerns should be eating well, staying away from harmful activities, and taking care of yourself. To lighten the load off your shoulders, I even recommend passing this book on to your birth partner or closest family member. This way you can both be aware of the best way to take care of you and the baby.

I've walked you through the details of each and every trimester. By now, you'll know all about your expected symptoms and you'll have picked up some tricks about how to manage them. You'll know what supplements to include in your diet, how to control your pregnancy weight, and how to take care of your skin to minimize the chance of stretch marks. In the early days, your body will be going through some big adjustments; by now, you'll know what these changes are. If you feel like you need someone else on board for some extra support, go ahead and begin the search for a doula! Especially for a first-time mom, a doula can make a world of difference to your first pregnancy experience.

Remember to start your pelvic floor exercises in the second trimester – that is, if you've decided to do them. It's completely optional, but they'll be highly valuable in preventing incontinence. Preeclampsia symptoms can show up as early as the second trimester, so if you notice any unusual symptoms, refer back to the preeclampsia section to see how many signs you check off. You're probably okay, but reach out to a doctor immediately if you're unsure. It's always best to be safe!

When the third trimester rolls around, it's about time to start preparing for your big day and your new life with your baby. Decide whether you'd like to breastfeed or formula-feed your baby. Make sure you have everything or at least most of the things on the 'Necessities' list. You won't want to go out shopping when your newborn arrives, so it's best to get that out of the way now! You can also prepare for your big day by creating a birth plan, but this isn't necessary. It's just a way for you to establish what you want for your big day and to ensure those wishes are met.

If you have a doula, she'll be able to tell you when you're in labor and when you need to go to the hospital. If you don't, then make sure you pay close attention to what the most common labor signals are. You should also know how to tell the difference between Braxton Hicks contractions and real labor contractions. You don't want to end up going to the hospital for nothing!

Eventually, your big day will come and your little one will be ready to be born. Whether you plan on a vaginal birth or a C-section, childbirth is rarely easy. Stay fully informed about what you can expect. If you're having a vaginal birth, read up on epidurals so you know whether you'd like one. Keep in mind that you may change your mind at the last minute, if the pain is intense. There's nothing wrong with this!

You'll feel a rollercoaster of emotions in the days following your child's birth. There will be overwhelming joy, but many mothers also develop the baby blues and postpartum depression. Don't feel guilty or ashamed if you have your low moments. This is normal. Seek out help if you feel you may have postpartum depression. It's easily treated in this day and age. Take care of your emotional health and also take care of your physical well-being. Do not stress your body out or perform rigorous exercise for a while. Focus on eating well, sleeping, and nursing your baby. Get all the help you need from your friends and family. And remember that self-care is extremely important for the recovering first-time mom!

Of course, the journey doesn't end once you give birth. This may seem like a lot already, but all of this counts as step one. Motherhood begins here. When you have your newborn baby in your arms, it'll feel like a new day has started and in many ways, it has. No mother will ever be 100% prepared because every baby is different, so when all else fails, focus on the core things: baby's food, sleep, and safety – and yours as well. You're not alone in this! Refer back to this book whenever you need to and don't be afraid to ask your partner for help.

Welcome to the beautiful and empowering journey of motherhood, first-time mom! You've done an incredible job. I wish you and your new family happiness, health, and a lifetime of fun adventures together.

First-Time Mom

30 Day Meal Plan

Week 1

	Breakfast	Lunch	Dinner
Day 1	Oatmeal with blueberries, sliced apple, and a pinch of cinnamon.	A peanut butter and banana sandwich made with whole-wheat bread.	Salmon with a side of baked broccoli and potatoes.
Day 2	Greek yogurt and berries of choice.	A cooked-turkey wrap with swiss cheese, avocado, spinach, and hummus.	Cooked shrimp (deveined and peeled) with broccoli, cauliflower, garlic, and tomatoes in olive oil.
Day 3	A smoothie made of bananas, raspberries, chia seeds, and low-fat vanilla yogurt.	A baked potato with butter and cheddar cheese.	Pasta in a light olive oil or butter sauce with spinach, mushrooms, and pine nuts, topped with parmesan cheese.
Day 4	An omelette with cheddar cheese and toasted whole-wheat bread, lightly buttered.	An arugula and fig salad topped with balsamic vinegar, walnuts, and parmesan.	Pork chops, green beans, and mashed sweet potatoes.
Day 5	Granola with low-fat yogurt and berries of choice.	A spinach and cheese quiche with any salad of choice.	Chicken tenders in a lemon sauce, topped with parmesan, with a side of brussel sprouts.

Day 6	A peanut butter, banana, milk, and spinach smoothie.	Avocado toast with a sprinkle of salt and pepper.	Roasted chicken with baked baby potatoes, asparagus, and carrots.
Day 7	Broccoli and cheddar cheese omelette.	Creamy butternut squash soup.	Garlic, shrimp, and mushroom quinoa cooked in vegetable broth.

Week 2

	Breakfast	Lunch	Dinner
Day 8	Scrambled eggs on whole-wheat toast with baked beans on the side.	A chicken salad with sliced avocado, spinach, parmesan, olive oil, and balsamic vinegar.	Beef liver, onions, and mushrooms with a side of brown rice.
Day 9	Oatmeal with two sliced bananas.	An egg wrap with cheddar cheese, spinach, and salsa.	Chicken cutlets in a mushroom sauce with peas and carrots.
Day 10	A smoothie made of bananas, pears, chia seeds, and low-fat vanilla yogurt.	Broccoli and pea soup with optional whole-wheat toast for dipping.	Lamb chops with a side of asparagus and sweet potato wedges.
Day 11	Greek yogurt and berries of choice.	A baked potato with cottage cheese.	Broccoli, spinach, and sweetcorn pasta bake with cheese.

Day 12	Spinach and cottage cheese omelette.	A peanut butter and banana sandwich made with whole-wheat bread.	Chicken soup with carrots and celery.
Day 13	Low-fat yogurt with sliced mango and banana.	A cooked-turkey wrap with swiss cheese, avocado, spinach, and hummus.	Salmon with a side of kale cooked in lemon and garlic.
Day 14	Granola with low-fat yogurt and berries of choice.	Spinach and edamame salad with grated carrots, parmesan shavings, and sweet corn with a citrus dressing.	Mushroom and chicken risotto made with brown rice.

Week 3

	Breakfast	Lunch	Dinner
Day 15	A smoothie made of kale, avocado, bananas, pineapple, and chia seeds.	A baked sweet potato stuffed with spinach, avocado, and topped with a sunny side up egg.	Pesto pasta with garlic, peas, and sun-dried tomatoes.
Day 16	Whole-wheat waffles topped with honey and sliced banana.	A walnut, pear, and feta cheese (pasteurized) salad.	Spaghetti bolognese.
Day 17	Sunny side up eggs with a side of mushrooms,	Lentil soup with carrots, garlic, potatoes, carrots,	Garlic, shrimp, and mushroom quinoa cooked in

	spinach, and tomatoes.	and parmesan shavings on top.	vegetable broth.
Day 18	Broccoli and cheddar cheese omelette.	Creamy butternut squash soup.	Chicken thighs baked with artichoke, peas, garlic, and onions.
Day 19	Whole-wheat toast with banana and peanut butter or other nut butter.	Feta, spinach, and mushroom quiche.	Pork chops, green beans, and mashed sweet potatoes.
Day 20	A peanut butter, banana, milk, and spinach smoothie.	A chicken salad with sliced avocado, spinach, parmesan, olive oil, and balsamic vinegar.	Grilled salmon in a buttery lemon sauce with a side of chopped baby potatoes and asparagus.
Day 21	Avocado toast with a sprinkle of salt and pepper.	An egg wrap with cheddar cheese, spinach, and salsa.	A mushroom, spinach, celery, and cheese pasta bake.

Week 4

	Breakfast	Lunch	Dinner
Day 22	Spinach and cottage cheese omelette.	An arugula and fig salad topped with balsamic vinegar, walnuts, and parmesan.	Meatballs in tomato sauce with a side of mashed potatoes and broccoli.

Day 23	Oatmeal with blueberries, sliced apple, and a pinch of cinnamon.	Broccoli and pea soup with optional whole-wheat toast for dipping.	Chicken tenders in a lemon sauce, topped with parmesan, with a side of brussel sprouts.
Day 24	Sunny side up eggs with a side of mushrooms, spinach, and tomatoes.	A peanut butter and banana sandwich made with whole-wheat bread.	Cooked shrimp (deveined and peeled) with broccoli, cauliflower, garlic, and tomatoes in olive oil.
Day 25	Granola with low-fat yogurt and berries of choice.	A baked sweet potato stuffed with spinach, avocado, and topped with a sunny side up egg.	Beef liver, onions, and mushrooms with a side of brown rice.
Day 26	Egg, bean, and cheese breakfast burrito.	Spinach and edamame salad with grated carrots, parmesan shavings, and sweet corn with a citrus dressing.	Mushroom and chicken risotto made with brown rice.
Day 27	A smoothie made of kale, avocado, bananas, pineapple, and chia seeds.	Avocado toast with a sprinkle of salt and pepper.	Chicken cutlets in a mushroom sauce with peas and carrots.
Day 28	Sliced peaches and mango in low-fat yogurt.	A pork and spinach salad with figs, red grapes, balsamic, honey, and pasteurized goat or	Pesto pasta with garlic, peas, and sun-dried tomatoes.

| | | feta cheese. | |

Week 5

	Breakfast	Lunch	Dinner
Day 29	Oatmeal with two sliced bananas.	Sandwich made of whole-wheat bread with artichoke, spinach, swiss cheese, sliced red peppers and sun-dried tomatoes.	Roasted chicken with baked baby potatoes, asparagus, and carrots.
Day 30	A peanut butter, banana, milk, and spinach smoothie.	Lentil soup with carrots, garlic, potatoes, carrots, and parmesan shavings on top.	Chicken thighs baked with artichoke, peas, garlic, and onions.

Snack List

Any Week

A bowl of mixed fruit	Chips and guacamole	Roasted tomatoes topped with parmesan	Banana bread
Cheese (pasteurized) and Crackers	Almonds	Kale chips	Dried fruit and nuts
One or two hard-boiled eggs	Cottage cheese	Cucumber and carrot sticks with peanut butter	Sweet potato chips
Edamame	Bananas	Low-fat yogurt and cereal fortified with iron or fiber	Hummus and pita bread
Homemade iced tea with lemon	Oatmeal and raisins	Orange slices	Black bean and cheese quesadilla

Enneagram Personality Types

Uncover Your Unique Path with The 9 Personality Types (#1 Made Easy Guide for Beginners)

Table of Contents

Introduction **120**
Chapter One - Understanding the Enneagram **123**
    What the Enneagram Figure Means 123
    How to Identify Your Personality Type 126
    About the Levels 127
Chapter Two - The Reformer (Type 1) **130**
    Fifteen Signs You're a Reformer 130
    The Reformer: An Overview 131
    The Reformer Levels 132
    The Reformer Wings 136
    Advice For The Reformer 138
Chapter Three – The Helper (Type 2) **141**
    Fifteen Signs You're a Helper 141
    The Helper: An Overview 142
    The Helper Levels 143
    The Helper Wings 145
    Advice for the Helper 147
Chapter Four – The Achiever (Type 3) **149**
    Fifteen Signs You're an Achiever 149
    The Achiever: An Overview 150
    The Achiever Levels 151
    The Achiever Wings 154
    Advice for the Achiever 156
Chapter Five - The Individualist (Type 4) **157**
    Fifteen Signs You're An Individualist 158
    The Individualist Overview 159
    The Individualist Levels 160

The Individualist Wings 163

Advice for The individualist 165

Chapter Six - The Investigator (Type 5) 166

Fifteen Signs You're An Investigator 166

The Inspector Overview 167

The Investigator Levels 168

The Investigator Wings 171

Advice for The Investigator 172

Chapter Seven - The Loyalist (Type 6) 174

Fifteen Signs You're A Loyalist 174

The Loyalist Overview 175

The Loyalist Levels 177

The Loyalist Wings 179

Advice for The Loyalist 181

Chapter Eight - The Enthusiast (Type 7) 183

Fifteen Signs You're an Enthusiast 183

The Enthusiast Overview 184

The Enthusiast Levels 185

The Enthusiast Wings 187

Advice for The Enthusiast 191

Chapter Nine - The Challenger (Type 8) 193

Fifteen Signs You're a Challenger 193

The Challenger Overview 194

The Challenger Levels 196

The Challenger Wings 198

Advice for The Challenger 201

Chapter Ten - The Peacemaker (Type 9) 203

Fifteen Signs You're a Peacemaker 203

The Peacemaker Overview... 205
The Peacemaker Levels.. 207
The Peacemaker Wings.. 210
Advice for The Peacemaker 212
Conclusion 214

Enneagram

Introduction

The world in which we live is a complex place, teeming with so many different voices, influences and ideas. It can be somewhat of a challenge to remain centered and stay true to who you are, to actually know and understand who you truly are, and take appropriate action based on this vital self-knowledge.

Do you seek clarity in a world that can often feel confusing? Would you like to grow personally, with the confidence that you are growing in the right direction? Perhaps you seek a better understanding of your loved ones. A way to avoid conflict and to achieve more harmony. To learn which partners you are compatible with and to deepen those relationships. If so, the Enneagram might well provide the solution you have been seeking.

Modern theories relating to the Enneagram are variously credited to the teachings of George Gurdjieff, Oscar Ichazo and Claudio Naranjo. It is a system of nine different personality types and it combines the considerable benefits of both modern psychology and traditional wisdom. It can be used as a powerful tool for understanding ourselves and others. It has also been used extensively in the realms of both spirituality and business - specifically in the areas of team building, leadership development and communication skills.

In this book, you will learn the basic tenets and principles of the Enneagram and receive thorough and revealing outlines of each individual personality type. You will discover your own particular 'type' along the way - there are nine in all - and the various strengths and challenges that accompany this. You will come to understand how to use these strengths to your advantage and how to overcome and transcend the unique issues that your particular type might have to grapple with.

For all of my life, I've held a deep passion for self-development and personality tests. It goes beyond everyday interest; my life has truly been shaped by my discoveries. And my deep understanding of the

Enneagram

Enneagram has allowed me to read people in a way that most people cannot. By identifying my personality type, I finally became able to identify my true needs. If you don't know what your needs are, how can you ever hope to meet them?

I have discovered from personal experience that by digging deep and learning who I truly am, my life is richer and more meaningful. I am also capable of making much better decisions when it comes to the more important things in life. I am an Enneagram Type Four and this knowledge helps me to know my frailties, to nimbly walk around them and to capitalize on and give myself credit for my strengths. In a way, it makes it easier when I know there is a reason for it all. It is not my fault, it is because I am a Four!

This book can be used as a guide along your road to self-discovery. You can use it as a tool to understand yourself more deeply and to identify your dominant traits. It provides everything you need to know on how to deal with all your wonderful idiosyncrasies and to achieve personal growth along the way. The book can provide additional insight too. By identifying the 'types' of our significant others - be they friends, partners or family members - we achieve a better insight into how to make these relationships work and furthermore, how to deepen them. Communication can be improved and conflicts lessened. People from all over the world and from every generation have given testimonials about the positive impact of the Enneagram on their lives. This can manifest in a whole range of ways. Examples include recognizing the mental patterns that underlie emotions. Developing self-awareness such as learning about the meaning of bodily sensations like tension. Understanding the strategies we use for self-preservation. Owning your own emotions and establishing boundaries. Allowing vulnerability and accessing your own innate wisdom.

This book provides a definitive guide to all you need to know about the Enneagram and how to utilize the knowledge it provides. You will discover your type. Learn your potential strengths and weaknesses. Gain access to the power of self-understanding. You will have a deeper analysis and insight into who you really are and into the personalities of all of those around you. Imagine how useful it would be to gain insight into your prickly co-worker or your difficult boss! And in your romantic life: picture the advantage you will have in assessing potential partners and even avoiding repeating unhealthy relationship patterns from your past.

Life is short. Why waste time in confusion when clarity can be yours? The Enneagram and the insights it reveals can be an excellent place to start. It is said that an unexamined life is not worth living. The Enneagram can provide the awareness that is ultimately the key to all change and leads to far reaching benefits.

Unconscious behaviours and triggers are brought to the fore, enabling us to finally deal with them. Not only can you grow personally, but you can improve your relationships, both in the workplace and with friends and loved ones.

The information pertaining to the Enneagram that is contained in this book has led to life changing and far reaching positive consequences for many. Join the growing ranks of people who have experienced wonderful changes in their friendships, careers, romantic relationships and personal development.

Two thousand years ago, as pilgrims approached the sacred temple at Delphi, they were greeted by the sign: "Know Thyself." This sage advice is just as relevant today. Self-knowledge is power. But first you have to seek it. Then use it. This book can help you do just that.

Chapter One - Understanding the Enneagram

There are many personality tests in the public domain. You may have heard of some of them. The Myers Briggs personality test is one of the most famous of these, and you might have taken this yourself. But I would venture to say that The Enneagram is more than a personality test. It would be more accurately described as an immensely powerful tool for personal, not to mention collective, transformation.

So just what is this enigma known as the Enneagram? To delve a little deeper into its true meaning and origins, we are first going to examine the symbol which represents it.

What the Enneagram Figure Means

The Enneagram symbol or figure is made up of three individual shapes, each having its own separate meaning. We will first examine the underlying circle:

The Circle

It will come as no surprise that the circle represents the wholeness or oneness of life - as in the Circle of Life. The circle also serves as a kind of container within which we conduct our lives. As we navigate our way through life, fragmentation can occur, often because of the ego. The goal is to reach awareness that we have never actually lost our wholeness.

The Triangle

In many cultures, three is regarded as a mystical and magical number. This is sometimes known as the Law of Threes. This law holds that every phenomenon consists of three individual forces. When three forces are present, things start to happen. But with only one or two forces available, nothing at all happens. Each force has a different name. The first is known as the active or positive or motivating force. The second one is called the negative or passive or denying force and the third is named the neutralizing, facilitating or invisible force. As an esoteric law, the Law of Threes works both in our inner world and our outer world. You might be able to observe it in your interactions with other people.

There are numerous cultural examples of the Law of Threes. One of the most pervasive and one which the majority of people will be familiar with, is that of the concept of the holy trinity - the father, son and The Holy Spirit - which is espoused by the Christian tradition.

The Hexad

The Hexad is a more unusual and irregular symbol which finds its origins in Sufism - the mystical branch of Islam. It is actually a six pointed figure but it follows seven points, from the start, through six changes of momentum, then back to its origin, which is considered the seventh point. It represents the Law of Seven, which is sometimes known as the law of octaves. It propounds that phenomena evolves in seven steps. Along with the Law of Threes, it was believed by Gurdjieff, a chief proponent of The Enneagram, that the Law of Seven was a global law and essential to his cosmology.

The Law of Seven states that the path of movement, either towards or away from anything, does not occur in a straight line. Rather, there are periods of striving, falling and striving again - a kind of rising and falling of energies along the way.

These three shapes are overlaid onto one another in order to create the Enneagram symbol. The lines on the Enneagram symbol show a path to a richer and fuller life. Self-observation is encouraged here, in order to avoid the different triggers of our personalities which might tend to lead one astray.

The numbers - one to nine - on the Enneagram symbol, represent the nine different personality types. The relationship between the numbers are demonstrated by the lines that connect them together. Each number is only connected to two other numbers.

<u>About the Wings</u>

No one person is made up purely of one personality type. Everyone is a mixture of their main type together with one of the two types next to it on the Enneagram figure. Whichever adjacent type that you most identify with is known as your 'wing.'

Your dominant wing is indicated by the higher score of one of the types that exists on either side of your basic type. For example, if your basic type is Three, your wing will be Two or Four, whichever one has the highest score. It is worth noting that the second highest overall score on your Enneagram test is not necessarily that of your wing.

The idea is that the wing types have an extra influence on your basic type.

The Triads (or Centers)

The nine personality types of the Enneagram are arranged into three triads, otherwise known as centers. Three of the types are in the instinctive center (One, Eight and Nine), three in the feeling center (Two, Three and Four) and three in the thinking center, (Five, Six and Seven). The three personalities that occupy the same center share the same strengths and weaknesses as one another.

Each triad or center is associated with a particular emotion. The instinctive center is associated with anger, whereas the feeling center tends to feel more shame. And the thinking center is linked to feelings of fear. Of course, each and every person can be subject to each and every emotion, but in each triad, the personalities associated with it are especially affected by that triad's emotional theme. You'll find that each personality type has a particular way of coping with its dominant emotion.

The three numbers within each triad or center have a pattern that they follow. The first number in each triad *expresses* the emotion that it is hyper-focused on. So types Eight, Two and Five express and externalize their emotions. This means that Eight externalizes anger, Two externalizes shame and Five externalizes fear.

This means that they either project the emotion outwardly or experience it outside themselves. When these personalities experience these emotions, they manifest right in front of us.

The second number in each center *represses* the emotion upon which it focuses. That is, Nine, Three and Six. So Nine represses anger, Three represses shame and Six represses fear. In other words, they do their best to pretend that the emotion doesn't exist for them.

The third number in each center *internalizes* the emotion it is most associated with. Thus, One, Four and Seven try to internalize their emotions. One internalizes anger, Four internalizes shame and Seven internalizes fear. These personalities experience these emotions inwardly or turn it in on themselves. This is different from repression because they still feel the emotion they are concealing, but they are choosing not to show it. This may lead these personality types, especially Four, to brood.

How to Identify Your Personality Type

The upcoming chapters provide a comprehensive guide to the nine different personality types, set out in numerical order. Each chapter begins with a check list comprising of fifteen questions to ask yourself in order to ascertain whether or not you are likely to be that particular type.

It would be a good idea to keep a record of which personality type you tick off the most statements for. This practice should identify your personality type. In a similar way, keep track of which adjacent personality type you score the most for. This will be your dominant wing.

It is quite common to find a little of yourself in all of the nine Enneagram personality types, although one of them should stand out as being the closest to you. This is your basic type.

We are all familiar with the ongoing debate between nature and nurture. In terms of the Enneagram, experts agree that we are born with a dominant type. This inborn temperament seems to determine the ways in which we adapt to our early childhood environment.

People do not switch from one personality type to another. For instance, if you are born a One, you will stay a One for the entirety of your life. A few other points are worth bearing in mind. All the types apply equally to men and to women. And a larger number on the Enneagram scale is no better or worse than a lower number. In other words, an eight is no better than a three or vice versa. Each type has its own inherent strengths and weaknesses. No Enneagram personality type is better or worse than another. We should all strive to be our best selves rather than striving to emulate other types.

About the Levels

Of course, not all the people from the same type will be exactly the same. This is obvious when we consider the diversity of the human beings we are surrounded with. So what is it that accounts for these differences?

Each personality type is made up of nine levels of development. This hypothesis was first reached by Don Riso in 1977. Riso, together with Russ Hudson, further developed the idea in the 1990s. The concept of the levels adds depth to our understanding of the Enneagram system and accounts both for the differences that arise between people of the same type and also how people can change, positively or negatively.

The levels of development provide deeper understanding to the explanation of the different elements contained within a personality type. This ties in with the complexity of human nature. The levels of development provide for us a kind of skeletal framework which allows us to see how all the traits of a particular type are interrelated, and how a healthy trait can become average, or can become unhealthy. Of course, this can work in the opposite direction also.

The levels show us that the personality is dynamic and ever changing. It helps us understand that people can change states within their personality, shifting within the spectrum of traits that make up their personality type.

It can help significantly in our understanding of others to assess whether someone is in their healthy, average or unhealthy level of functioning.

The nine levels of development are comprised of three levels in the healthy segment, three levels in the average segment and three levels in the unhealthy segment. Shades of grey abound.

The continuum of the levels of development is as follows:

Healthy
Level 1: The level of liberation
Level 2: The level of psychological capacity
Level 3: The level of social value

Average
Level 4: The level of imbalance/social role
Level 5: The level of interpersonal control
Level 6: The level of overcompensation

Unhealthy
Level 7: The level of violation
Level 8: The level of obsession and compulsion
Level 9: The level of pathological destructiveness

Try and be as honest as you can when it comes to assessing your own level. Even though this can sometimes expose uncomfortable truths, it is the surest path to personal growth.

Levels can be understood in terms of our capacity to be present. The further we move down the levels, the less present we are and the more we are identified with the ego and its negative patterns. The lower down the levels we go, the more defensive, compulsive and destructive we become. We tend to be less free, less self-aware, and act on a more sub-conscious level.

Conversely, as we move up the levels, we become more and more present. We are less destructive and increasingly free and open. We are far more self-aware and astute. We are less likely to get caught up in negativity.

Becoming more present allows us to be more objective about our personality and we become adept at self-observation. This makes us more effective in all areas of our lives, whether that be relationships or our career. It can bring genuine peace and joy to whatever it is that we are doing.

Chapter Two - The Reformer (Type 1)

Also known as the Perfectionist

Fifteen Signs You're a Reformer

1. You strive to make the world a better place in which to live. You are capable of seeing, in clear detail, what is wrong with a situation and you are prepared to take the necessary steps to rectify matters.

2. You possess a very strong sense that you have a life purpose or a mission to fulfill.

3. Other people often describe you as being responsible, dependable and brimming over with common sense. They can also sometimes accuse you of having no feelings. (You *do* have feelings – you're just keeping them all in!)

4. You think you have to do everything perfectly, going so far as to think that *you* yourself have to be perfect.

5. You are highly self-disciplined - sometimes to a fault. You have little to no trouble sticking to a schedule or routine.

6. You hate feeling stagnant and you always ache to be useful in some way.

7. You feel you have to keep a lid on all your very strong wants and needs.

8. It is vitally important to you that you 'do the right thing.'

9. You have an intense fear of making mistakes or blunders.

10. You tend to experience tension in your shoulders, neck and jaw.

11. It sometimes takes you longer than the average person to complete a task, which is, of course, because of your exceptional eye for detail.

12. You can be very critical of yourself and others.

13. You may experience disappointment and frustration at those times when reality does not meet your expectations.

14. You hold yourself to very high standards of excellence.

Does this sound anything like you?

The Reformer: An Overview

Perfectionism can be a double-edged sword. On the one hand, it can cause impressive and wonderfully satisfying results. On the other, it can lead to wounding self-criticism and even inaction, where the perfectionist might not even begin a task for fear of failure.

Type One in The Enneagram model is not lacking in the least when it comes to admirable traits such as reliability, honesty, common sense, integrity and nobility. In fact, this type can be downright heroic. They could, however, learn to be kinder to themselves. Although lowering your standards is not usually to be recommended, Ones could sometimes benefit from taking such advice, as the expectations they heap upon themselves - and others - can be unrealistically and punishingly high.

This type wishes to make the world a better place, and what's not to like about that?! High ideals are the order of the day, coupled with a strong sense of purpose. These people get things done and done right! You might also recognize a One by their fastidious attention to detail: that go-to co-worker who you can always rely on. Granted, they may take longer than most to complete the task, but the end result will be undoubtedly flawless. Or it might be the friend with the incredible self-discipline, who will keep to the diet or the exercise regime and whose gym membership will be used beyond the third week in January.

If you want to keep in a One's good books, make sure you keep your promises. *Never* say you are going to do something and then back out or forget about it. This is a complete no-no and breaks their ethical code. These good people would never do the same to you! And don't forget to take things seriously. This type does not appreciate a flippant attitude. It will surprise and delight them if you join them in speculating about how things can be improved in the world, and you will make all their dreams come true by actually taking action. Encourage them also to be less critical of themselves. Teach them that a little self-kindness goes a long way. Above all, a One needs a friend who can coax them to have fun and to take life - and themselves - a little less seriously.

The Reformer Levels

Healthy
Heroism

Type Ones on The Enneagram are the stuff that heroes are made of. A man by the name of Gandhi comes to mind. He embodied the qualities of the One at his or her best, in his capacity for extraordinary wisdom and discernment. His humanity inspired immense loyalty and made him a great leader that thousands of people felt compelled to follow. And we need look no further than Joan of Arc for a historical example of a One who uplifted many and created change through the courage of her conviction and willingness to self sacrifice.

Not every One can be a Gandhi or a Joan of Arc, but within their own private sphere of influence, no matter how big or small, they can often perform acts of everyday heroism.

Practical Action
It is one thing to have lofty ideals. It is quite another to act in accordance with them. But the One is a master of practical action, striving always to be useful, to fix the things that they consider broken and to fulfil their powerful mission in life. These people put their money where their mouth is. They have no qualms around making personal sacrifices to serve a higher cause.

Loyalty
The Reformer will not say one thing and then do another. They are impeccable with their word. Neither will they make promises to do something and then not do it. If you are lucky enough to have the friendship of a One, you know that you have someone who will always have your back.

Attention to Detail
A One will not leave a job half-done. Neither will they turn in a shoddy project. They always strive for excellence, in thought, word and deed. This type is always pushing the envelope and raising standards - for themselves and the world in which they live. Consider these prominent Ones in the areas of politics, business and entertainment. Such people as: Nelson Mandela, Michelle Obama, Anita Roddick (The Body Shop), Martha Stewart, Dame Maggie Smith and Meryl Streep, Confucious, Margaret Thatcher, Plato, George Bernard Shaw, Noam Chomsky, Emma Thompson, Jane Fonda, Jerry Seinfeld, George Harrison, Hilary Clinton, Jimmy Carter, Prince Charles.

Integrity
A One's deep sense of integrity makes him or her an excellent teacher and, in general, a witness and proponent of the truth. They are principled to the core and will uphold these principles even at the cost of their own safety or comfort. You can trust them to always do the right thing, even if this goes against conventional wisdom or public

opinion. The Reformer will not be swayed from what he or she believes to be right and good.

Neutral or Average

Dissatisfaction
The Reformer at this level thinks it is up to them to fix everything. They feel they know how everything 'should' be done and that it is their absolute duty to tell everybody else what they should do too!

Rigidity

This rigidity is caused by the fear of making a mistake. Everything has to be exactly right. There is no margin for error whatsoever, either for the Reformer themselves or for those around them.

Overly critical
The Reformer directs this criticism - not just at him or herself - but at others too. They feel the need to correct people constantly, and not in an especially sensitive way! Very low level of satisfaction.

Unhealthy

Hell is other people!
It's not always easy being a Reformer. You will constantly encounter those with different value systems to your own and this might well upset your high-minded ideals and insistence on excellence. It may lead you to be self-righteous, intolerant, dogmatic or inflexible. You might severely judge others for their inability to see things in the same way that you do.

Obsession
There is a risk that Ones can become obsessive in nature. This can manifest itself in a number of ways. One of these is in the area of diet

and nutrition. In extreme cases, the Reformer's quest for self-control might lead to conditions such as anorexia and bulimia. Some might also resort to alcohol in order to alleviate the stress that they put themselves under. Obsessive Compulsive Disorder is also a danger to this type.

Anger
The Reformer can get angry very easily and this anger can often have a tinge of self-righteousness to it. Offense may be taken easily, from other people's refusal to do what the One believes to be right. This anger - however righteous - can unfortunately have the effect of alienating others. This is a great pity, as Ones often have a very valid point to make. Repressing this anger is not the answer either, as this might manifest in health issues such as high blood pressure or ulcers.

Depression
This is a fate that can befall a person with a dominant Type One personality, when the trait takes an unhealthy turn. A less than healthy Reformer can be extremely condemnatory, not to mention cruel, to themselves and others. Depressions, breakdowns and suicide attempts are the worst possible outcome here.

Unrealistically High Standards
Enneagram Type Ones can struggle with intense disappointment when reality does not match up to their expectations. It can make them appear overly negative or critical of other family members, friends or co-workers. It can make them very harsh task masters - pedantic and unforgiving. It is not pleasant to be on the receiving end of an unhealthy One's constant criticism and disappointment at your efforts.

But it's not all doom and gloom!

So, if you are a One - a Perfectionist, a Reformer - how can you best avoid the potential pitfalls and instead bring out the best in what your personality type has to offer?

The Reformer Wings

Type One with a Two wing (1W2)
What do you get when you cross a Type One with a Type Two? Well, for a start, the One becomes less repressed and a little more emotionally balanced by the two's directedness and desire to please others.

This is often a very neat and tidy-looking person. The One gives them a propensity for perfectionism and the Two makes them more sensitive to criticism. In other words, they don't want to be criticized about their appearance. So their hair will be perfect and clothing will be just so. They might hold themselves very correctly and come across as having rather a condescending attitude.

This subtype is very hard on his or herself. They will make every effort to do the right thing and if they can also manage to please others in the process, that's even more preferable.

The healthy version of a One with a Two wing is a more relaxed version of a full One with less of an inclination to be righteously judgmental. They can actually believe and admit that they might not always be right!

The One enjoys correcting others. With the influence of the Two, the corrections become more helpful and less intrusive. They are also better able to tolerate differences with the benefit of the Two wing.

If the Reformer with the Two wing happens to experience a kind of spiritual awakening, he or she can become a most inspiring teacher who can bring joy and compassion to their practice. One is wise and

Two is loving. At their best, this sub type can be a sterling friend who always seems to know the right thing to say or do.

But oh dear! Things can take a turn for the worse when the Reformer's not so emotionally healthy and mature. The One's perfectionism combined with the Two's pride can lead to trouble. It can amount to great inner conflict. Self-critical introspection goes into overdrive and may be accompanied by fits of rage which descend into self-judgement and remorse.

When severely unhealthy, the anger and pride combine to create despair. Here, the One with a Two wing will punish themselves endlessly and suicide might even be the end result.

It is not surprising the Reformer with a Two wing might enjoy work that involves helping other people become perfect. Examples of such would be teachers, dieticians and judges.

Type One with a Nine wing (1W9)
The combination of the perfectionism and judgement of Type One with the withdrawal from stress of Type Nine makes for a quiet, conservative and somewhat repressed sub type. They do not show a lot of emotion and they will come across as quite strict, quiet and practical. They are slow to express their views also but will usually act from principled judgement.

They can, of course, shine when emotionally healthy and mature. Here, they will learn to access an inner warmth and be capable of bringing it to the fore. Although they might still be a little judgmental, they allow for the fact that they are capable of getting it wrong at times. And anyway, it doesn't really matter that much after all. They learn at this stage to control the propensity of the Nine to withdraw under stress and this allows them to participate in life more fully. They are gentle, responsible, fun-loving and capable of relaxing and just letting go.

At their very best, they will be ever more joyful and participate in life with much gusto. They will have high self-esteem at this level. The wisdom of the One will merge with the selflessness of the Nine and can allow them to obtain significant spiritual advancement.

But this sub type can be unhealthy too and when they are, they might try to exert too much control over their emotions which will lend to them a physical rigidity punctuated by fissions of explosive energy.

Repressed emotions are ever present under the surface and they will come across as "nervy" types. They will be hostile and withdrawn and suffer from self-hatred. They might be highly suspicious and engage in passive-aggressive behaviour. Most of this will be bottled up.

If things disintegrate even further, they can come across as robotic and ritualistic. Anxiety about performing routines just right can become extreme. They may descend into psychosis and become paralyzed with inaction.

This variant of the One stands upright and offers few, but genuine, smiles. It is possible that they are drawn to work that expresses their talent for performing precise tasks, such as accountancy or computer programming.

Advice For The Reformer

I know you didn't ask for advice, but we're going to give it to you anyway! As a Reformer, you probably don't feel you need any counsel, because of your higher than average sense of right and wrong and your intense feeling of purpose. And you are right, to a point. We each need to follow our own star. However, we all have our weaknesses too, and it can be very useful at times to have a second eye, as it were, to give us a greater sense of perspective.

1. Keep in mind that not everyone will see the world in such black and white terms as you do. There are numerous shades of grey and sometimes you need to make allowances for middle-ground.

2. Find a healthy way to express and release your anger, one that doesn't involve another human having to feel the full extent of

your wrath but at the same time, means you don't repress it all, which could lead to serious health problems for you. It may also help to find less reasons to be angry. Accepting other people's imperfections, perhaps! Don't forget that people can be chaotic. If someone turns up late for an appointment, it doesn't necessarily mean that they disrespect you or don't value your time. They might just be struggling with the messiness of their own lives. Be less critical of others. And while you're at it, be less critical of yourself too!

3. Keep in mind the famous serenity prayer: Grant me the serenity to accept the things I cannot change, the courage to change the things I can and the wisdom to know the difference.

4. Be cognizant that you have a tendency to store tension in your body, particularly in your jawline, neck and shoulders. Consider taking steps to counteract this, such as meditation, massage or other relaxation techniques. And why not try to have fun! This is a proven and excellent path to relaxation. After all, nobody likes a martyr!

5. It is possible that you had parents with very high expectations of you. If this is the case, perhaps it is now time to re-parent yourself and show yourself more softness and kindness. Remember: 'Angels fly because they take themselves lightly.' You don't have to take yourself so seriously all the time. And remind yourself often that everyone makes mistakes, including you. You are not a failure if you make a mistake. This is how we learn. Acceptance of this is key. Furthermore, it is perfectly acceptable to have human emotions and impulses. And sometimes 'good enough' is good enough. Perfection is an illusion. So forgive yourself for your imperfections. Forgiveness is a gift to yourself even more so than to the one that you are forgiving.

6. You often feel that the weight of the world is on your shoulders. Thankfully, it is not. You are just one person and you are doing just fine.

7. Trust your inner guidance and most of all, trust life.. Your tendency to see so clearly where things need to be improved, can make you blind to the many things that are right with the world. If you look more closely, you will recognize that things are often working out.

8. Try not to be too disappointed or impatient if those around you don't change immediately in accordance with what you might have taught them. It does not mean that you are not a gifted teacher, but rather that everyone develops at their own pace. Patience is a virtue!

Above all, don't stop being who you are. There is a reason you were born this way so find out why and make the most of it!

Chapter Three – The Helper (Type 2)

Also known as the Giver

Fifteen Signs You're a Helper

1. You love to be involved in other people's lives.

2. You always feel the urge to put other people before yourself.

3. You tend to give a lot of time and money to charity.

4. You are able to see the good in your fellow humans.

5. You need to be needed.

6. You can totally exhaust yourself, running around doing things for other people.

7. You may feel offended if someone refuses your offer of help.

8. You require appreciation for the things you do for others.

9. Your friends describe you as being someone who is always willing to go that extra mile.

10. You sometimes forget to look after yourself and this can lead to physical or emotional burnout.

11. You don't consider life worth living unless you are giving to others in some way.

12. You have a deep seated fear of worthlessness.

13. You might well be a wonderful cook and homemaker!

14. You might have a tendency to use food to 'stuff' down your feelings.

15. Personal relationships are of the utmost importance to you.

Do any of the above points ring a bell?

The Helper: An Overview

The focus of Type Two of the Enneagram is very much on relationships. It is what makes these people tick - making connections and then empathizing with the feelings and needs of others. However, they can go too far in this tendency and can twist themselves into all sorts of shapes just to win approval from their peers. Co-dependency is a trap that type two can sometimes fall prey to, priding themselves on what they can do for other people and feeling shame at those times when they can't actually help or support others.

In a way, our culture nurtures and awards the typical behavior of a Type Two, in that it encourages us to believe that our self-worth comes from what we do for other people. Women especially are taught this kind of behaviour. Although being kind to others is, of course, laudable, the Helper must guard against a tendency to smother or overwhelm. And it is never good for someone to deny their own personal interests and needs. Burnout or martyrdom may ensue! So if you are a Two, you would do well to balance your impulse to assist others with your own self-care.

As a Helper, love is your highest goal. You pride yourself on selflessness. You are often extroverted and may also have the knack for creating a comfortable and welcoming home for your family. You are huge on empathy and often a genuinely caring person with a very warm heart. You are friendly and generous. Just make sure that your motives for helping others are pure.

Examples of famous twos include such luminaries as Bishop Desmond Tutu, Byron Katie, John Denver, Dolly Parton, Eleanor Roosevelt, Luciano Pavarotti, Stevie Wonder, Elizabeth Taylor, Martin Sheen, Bobby McFerrin, Lionel Richie, Nancy Reagan, Josh Groban, Paula Abdul and Barry Manilow.

Type two has been given the name 'The Helper' for a reason: these people are either the most genuinely helpful to others *or* the most in need to see themselves as helpful.

The Helper Levels

As with every other type, Helpers differ in maturity and psychological health. We will explore the state of The Helper at healthy, neutral and unhealthy stages.

Healthy
Unconditionally Loving
The Helper at his or her best is capable of giving truly unconditional love. He or she is humble and unselfish, feeling it is a privilege to give and to be meaningfully involved in the lives of others.

Empathetic
Empathy is the helper's middle name. This type can be spilling over with compassion and concern for their fellow human beings. In addition, they have learnt the art and value of forgiveness.

Encouraging
The Helper at this level can easily appreciate the goodness of other people. They have learnt to balance service with self-care and give for all the right reasons.

Neutral
The People-Pleaser

An air of desperation can sometimes creep into Type Two's desire to help others. A kind of clinging rather than closeness. They might be tempted to give compliments that are not entirely genuine but instead meant to gain favor from the person they are flattering.

The Co-Dependent

This stage involves possessiveness and intrusiveness. The need to be needed can become so strong that the Type Two can be deeply controlling yet tell themselves that they are actually being loving. They want others to be dependent on them and often wear themselves out with needlessly self-sacrificial behaviour.

Self-Importance

A heightened sense of self-importance is probable at this level. Martyrdom can really kick in with the Helper believing that they are being far more helpful than they actually are! Type Two at this level might feel that he or she is indispensable when they are really not, and this can cause them to be patronizing and overbearing.

Unhealthy
Manipulation

Oh dear! Things start to get nasty when Type Twos exhibit unhealthy behavior patterns. At this level, a Two may well pile on the guilt, highlighting how much they believe people owe them for all they've done. This level displays the general attitude of "How *could* you after everything I've done for you?!" If people do not show the requisite level of appreciation, they might undermine them in an aggressive way. At this level, the Two will lack the self-awareness to see how unreasonable and damaging their behavior is. They may also begin to use food and drugs as a way of self-medication.

Domineering

At this unsavory level, the Two feels that everybody they've "helped" - whether or not that person asked for that help in the first place or actually wanted it at all! - owes them an enormous debt of gratitude and therefore must "pay" in whatever way the Two deems appropriate. There is a negative sense of entitlement where this type asserts the hold they feel they have earned.

Chronic Resentment
Such resentment arises when an unhealthy Two steps fully into victim mode and feels unjustly abused by those they have "helped." Because of this, they feel justified in displaying all sorts of irrational and aggressive behavior. All these highly negative emotions can result in serious health problems, both physical and mental. Not a happy place to be! Both for the Helper and for those around them.

The Helper Wings

As previously discussed, a type's wings are derived from the two number types that are physically beside it on the circumference of the Enneagram figure. For the Helper, the Reformer (Type 1) and the Achiever (Type 3) are possible wings or influencers on the personality.

Type Two with a One Wing (2W1)
We have already seen that Type Ones are perfectionists at heart. On the plus side, they are responsible, conscientious, progress-oriented and potentially heroic. Their shadow side can be hyper-critical, this being directed both at themselves and others. At times, they can also be resentful and judgemental. So what can a Type Two with a One wing look like?

All going well, this combination of types leads to a person who is loving, warm and generous, as you would expect, but the One influence adds resolve and moral obligation. The desire to do good is thus heightened by the number One's motivation to do everything 'right.'

The focus of the One's generosity becomes a drive for social justice under the influence of the Reformer. The desire to improve the world is genuine. The Helper with this wing is also more willing to take on the unglamorous tasks that other people usually eschew, for the sake of the common good. The influence of the One on the Two can imbue them with a stronger backbone and a better awareness of where feelings might threaten to overtake their good judgment.

But, as always, there is a flip side. Destructive perfectionism could rear its ugly head, causing the helper to think that they, and they alone, know best. This makes them imposing, preachy and intrusive. They may also judge themselves very severely. A potential negative side of this combination of types can also be that the Two has even more trouble recognizing her own needs and feelings and strongly believes that her own personal desire is selfish and should be quashed.

Type Two with a Three Wing (1W3)

We will examine Type Three in detail later on. For the time being, here is a brief summary:

Type Three is variously known as the Achiever or the Performer. As the name suggests, these people tend to be ambitious, enthusiastic and adaptable. They are driven and like nothing more than to accomplish goals and receive validation from others.

A Three wing makes the Two more social and good-humored than a One wing tends to do. It is all about the heart and feelings when it comes to this pairing. Relationships are sought and valued. This combination of types often possesses much charisma and others enjoy their company greatly. They are natural and gracious hosts or hostesses and love to throw parties and gather friends together for celebrations. They have great generosity of spirit and love to give of themselves for the betterment of others.

In times of stress, however, the 2W3, who perceives other's feelings so strongly, can be overwhelmed by the needs of others and even their own repressed emotions. Because types Two and Three both belong in the heart-centered triad, they lack the self-awareness that the influence of a head or body (such as One) type would lend to them. This particular marriage of types can lead to over-sensitivity if they are on the receiving end of criticism. Their sense of pride can become over-inflated, which might lead to authoritarian behaviour and outbursts of anger.

Advice for the Helper

1. Take care to look after your own self-care. You are so busy empathizing with other people and supporting them in their needs, that you forget your own needs in the process. Your own requirements are just as important as everybody else's. It is important to set and maintain your own personal boundaries and to ensure that you get adequate rest, exercise and proper nutrition. Do not change yourself in order to win approval from another. By being yourself and establishing boundaries, you can give to others more authentically, and you can only be of real service to others if you are balanced, healthy and centered within yourself.

2. Before you help somebody, consider whether or not they actually need or want your help in the first place. Have they asked for your assistance? Make sure that you are not just imposing your ideas of the way things should be upon them and interfering unnecessarily. Furthermore, it is not up to you to demand gratitude or decide the manner in which such gratitude is expressed. Instead, try asking people directly what it is they really need. Just because you can sense the need of another, does not necessarily mean that they would like you to step in and 'solve' all their problems for them. You must be willing to accept a "no, thank you" if that is what's forthcoming. This should not be taken as rejection.

3. In the event of you doing something nice for someone, there is no need whatsoever to remind them of it. This is a temptation you need to resist. It will only make the other party question your motivation for helping them in the first place and will cause them to be uncomfortable. They might also withdraw from you altogether, if you choose to behave in this way. Let kindness be its own reward!

4. Understand that people express their affection and appreciation in lots of different ways. Just because it is in a manner that is not instantly recognizable to you and not necessarily a way which you would have chosen yourself, does not mean that they do not care. Learn to recognize the different manifestations of love.

5. Make sure you are honest about your own motives and that you are not lying to yourself about why you are helping someone. If you are just doing it in order to receive gratitude, this is not a healthy motive and you might well be setting yourself up for disappointment. You must guard against co-dependency at all times.

Chapter Four – The Achiever (Type 3)

Also known as the Performer

Fifteen Signs You're an Achiever

1. You like to get things done and are more than willing to work hard to achieve your goals.

2. You can find it hard to slow down and you might struggle to find time to relax.

3. Patience is not one of your virtues!

4. Those around you describe you as a "Type A" personality.

5. You tend to store tension in your chest and heart area.

6. You have no problem setting aside your hobbies to chase success in your primary goal.

7. You love a challenge and relish throwing everything you have into meeting that challenge.

8. If at first you don't succeed, you will try, try, try again.

9. Your biggest fear is failure and this can cause you much stress and anxiety.

10. You focus on appearance. You can become overly concerned with your image and how other people perceive you.

11. A question you are often asked is, "How do you achieve so much?"

12. You very much enjoy a sense of completion and accomplishment. There's nothing like ticking boxes off your to-do list!

13. You are highly competitive and this is something that drives you.

14. You are 'self-made' in some way, having got to where you are in life by hard work and determined pursuit of your goals.

15. You have a lot of energy and others might describe you as having a zest for life which they often find attractive.

What do you think? Have many of the above points resonated with you?

The Achiever: An Overview

As the name suggests, the Type Three on the Enneagram is all about success. It is of vital importance to this type that their success is acknowledged. The Achiever requires this validation in order to feel worthy. They are highly focused, hard-working and competitive. These goals are often in the business world but they are not restricted to this sphere by any means. The Three is commonly a 'self-made' success, often skilled in the art of networking. Generally extroverted, the Achiever can sometimes be charismatic. There is a boundless energy and plenty of drive. Their shadow side is their secret fear of failure.

The Achiever, or the Performer, is frequently image-conscious and as such, can be slow to let his or her real self be shown. This can make intimacy difficult. The Three fears others getting too close lest they discover what they are *really* like.

Because of the Type Three's strong requirement for external validation, they sometimes make the error of chasing external success while ignoring their deeper needs and desires. The Achiever needs to guard against falling in to such a trap.

Notable Three's from the worlds of history, politics, sports and the arts include Bill Clinton, Arnold Schwarzenegger, Oprah Winfrey, Madonna, Lady Gaga, Will Smith, Augustus Caesar, Tony Blair, Andy Warhol, Elvis Presley, Barbra Streisand, Richard Gere, Reese Witherspoon, Anne Hathaway, Justin Bieber, Jon Bon Jovi, Paul McCartney, Lance Armstrong, O.J,Simpson, Truman Capote, Muhammad Ali, Emperor Constantine, Prince William, Carl Lewis, Tony Robbins, Deepack Chopra, Michael Jordan, Sting, Brooke Shields, Tiger Woods, Taylor Swift, Tom Cruise, Demi Moore, Courtney Cox and Kevin Spacey.

The Achiever Levels

Healthy

Authenticity
So genuine and appealing, the Three at their best is literally dripping with gentleness and benevolence. They have learned to fully accept themselves and to listen to their own internal guidance systems. These Threes are everything they appear to be as they have come to understand that they have nothing to hide. They are modest when it comes to their innate strengths and achievements and they are typically big-hearted people with a delightfully self-deprecating humour.

Competence
The high self-esteem of a healthy Three assists them in believing in themselves and their own capabilities. This type is self-assured with plenty of energy to get the job done and get it right. There is an intrinsic self-belief and a deep awareness of their own value as human beings. They are competent and confident enough to adapt to all sorts of

situations and remain gracious and charming in the process. Many people will be naturally drawn to a healthy Three.

Ambitious
These Threes are ambitious in the very best sense of the word. Never ruthless, just eager to be the best version of themselves and to fulfill their potential. Self-improvement is a driving force for these people. The healthy Achiever has it in him or her to become an outstanding human, possessing a tremendous amount of admirable qualities. Other people tend to admire them greatly and try to emulate them. This makes the healthy Three a master motivator.

Neutral
Driven
The average Type Three sets great store in doing their job well. Unfortunately, at this level, their motivation for this can be slightly less healthy and based more frequently on an abject terror of failure. They worry very much about what other people think of them and base their self-worth on the achievement of goals. It is said that comparison is the thief of joy. It certainly is for this type. This less than healthy Three will compare his or herself with others in a quest for their own status and self-worth. This is the level of the social climber or the one who believes that a career is everything.

Image-Consciousness
The Achiever can care far too much about how he or she is perceived by others. This can cause them to be "phony" in some ways as they try to conform with the real or imagined expectations of others. They can certainly excel in practicality and efficiency but they risk losing touch with their feelings in their desire to impress. This can lead to issues with intimacy.

Self-Promotion

The intense desire to impress others can cause the Three, at this level of maturity, to promote themselves ceaselessly and aggressively. They might elevate their achievements to this cause. It might feel a little like the childish tendency to say "look at me!" Inflated notions of themselves may arise and they may come across as arrogant and full of contempt, but this is just an attempt to disguise their jealousy.

Unhealthy
Fear of Failure
The Achiever at this level is willing to do or say whatever they consider necessary to preserve their image. Fear of failure and humiliation is intense at this point and can lead them to exploitative and opportunistic behaviours. They will be extremely jealous of another person's success and will strive to preserve their fragile illusion of superiority at all costs.

Deception
These folks can become so terrified at the thought of their mistakes and misdeeds being exposed that they will resort to all sorts of devious behaviours to cover up such failings. This means, of course, that the Achiever at this unhealthy level can absolutely not be trusted. They might betray or sabotage somebody just to get one up on them and their jealous states can border on delusional.

Narcissism
This is the Three at their absolute worst, when their actions correspond with the description of the Narcissistic Personality Disorder. They will stop at nothing to ruin another person's happiness and their destructiveness can become obsessive. The vindictiveness of the profoundly unhealthy Three can border on the psychopathic.

The Achiever Wings

Type Three with a Two Wing (3W2)
When you envisage the "typical" salesperson, you might well be picturing the Type Three with a Two wing. The Achiever's desire to be admired overtakes the Type Two's desire to please others and make them feel good. Although, if it's possible, they may well do both. This variety of the number Three is usually extroverted and can come across as attractive and even seductive. Their persona is cheerful and calm and they will be keen to show their best side and want to be perceived as having it together emotionally.

The influence of the Two wing on the Three personality, can make their "shine" more genuine. At best, this variety of the Three is big on self-observation and likely to be a humble type. They'll also be friendly and likeable with great social skills that cause others to enjoy being around them. The Two wing tempers the Three's hunger to always be the winner. Genuine feelings come to the fore and powerful bonds of friendship can and will be formed.

A healthy Type Three with a Two wing can become an excellent motivational speaker, capable of inspiring great confidence and optimism in others. Uplifting and positive - think Tony Robbins or Oprah Winfrey at their best.

However, when unhealthy, a brittle vanity can come into play for the Achiever with a Two wing. They can lose touch with their genuine innermost feelings while instead constructing a false emotional facade. Self-promotion can become pushy and aggressive, resulting in a lose-lose situation for all involved. They might appear nice and quiet on the outside but the internal reality could be quite unpleasant and destructive.

As outer appearance is important, the 3W2 will typically dress well and in accordance with the latest mainstream fashion. This is because they will want to appeal to the largest possible audience. They might be drawn to "glamorous" work - perhaps on stage, TV, radio, or a high profile position in the business world.

Type Three with a Four Wing (3W4)
Although the Achiever with a Four wing would still like to be admired, they would prefer that this be for their uniqueness rather than appealing to the general masses - a select following rather than mass appeal is what they are aiming for.
The Four wing will tend to make the Three more introverted and less comfortable in social situations, although because of the still dominant Type Three personality, they will be able to hide this with their social competence. They will still be able to hold it all together in times of pressure.
A healthy and mature Achiever with a Four wing is compassionate, gentle and competent. This variant is wise and socially responsible and highly effective in accomplishing their goals, all the while remaining intuitive. A suitable job for this type would be as a career counsellor or a business mentor.
At their absolute best, the Type Three with a Four wing is quietly self-assured while possessed of stunning emotional insight. They teach through example, influencing others through compassionate action. They can be found at the top of organizations or behind the scenes, inspiring others to perform their best.
It is an entirely different story when the Achiever with a Four wing is immature and unhealthy. A lack of balance here will make the Three-influenced drive for success compulsive, while at the same time causing the introspection of the Four to get out of hand. Manipulation comes to the fore and the desire to help is no longer coming from a good place. They are not so great socially and may also indulge in self-deception. They might feel a compulsive need to tell other people about their accomplishments. At their worst, they can be destructive to the self and others.
They like to appear both attractive and unique, wanting to be trend-setters rather than slavishly following the latest fashion. The 3W4

variant is typically drawn to quite showy professions, such as music, politics, broadcasting, the stage, the fashion industry and the sales side of business.

Advice for the Achiever

1. Take a break every now and then from the relentless pursuit of your goals! Your health will benefit and so will your levels of happiness. And let's not forget your loved ones, who will all be pleased to have more time with you. Your goals will still be waiting for you when you wake up from a good night's sleep or return from a holiday. And you will feel refreshed and more effective than ever. Not to mention, nicer to be around. Ambition and determination can be sterling qualities, but they must be tempered by periods of rest which, additionally, allow time for you to reconnect deeply with your inner needs and feelings.

2. Try to be completely honest with yourself. Threes can sometimes get so caught up in trying to play to the peanut gallery that they lose touch with what they really need to be happy. Take time to consider what success actually means to you. What are your values? What makes you happy? Only when you truly connect with the reality of who you are, can you achieve real freedom.

3. As intimacy can sometimes be a challenge for you, it is worth taking the time and trouble to connect with a few chosen people on a deeper level. This takes self-awareness and the willingness to relax and practice appreciation for those you love.

4. It will benefit you greatly to become involved in projects that are unrelated to your ultimate ambition or career goals. It will take you outside of yourself in a healthy way and transcend your preoccupation with the opinions of others.

Chapter Five - The Individualist (Type 4)

Also known as The Romantic

A short message from the Author:

Hey! Sorry to interrupt. I just wanted to check in and ask if you're enjoying the Enneagram audiobook? I'd love to hear your thoughts!
Many readers and listeners don't know how hard reviews are to come by, and how much they help an author.
So I would be incredibly thankful if you could take just 60 seconds to leave a quick review on Audible, even if it's just a sentence or two!
And don't worry, it won't interrupt this audiobook.
To do so, just click the 3 dots in the top right corner of your screen inside of your Audible app and hit the "Rate and Review" button.
This will take you to the "rate and review" page where you can enter your star rating and then write a sentence or two about the audiobook. It's that simple!
I look forward to reading your review. Leave me a little message as I personally read every review!
Now I'll walk you through the process as you do it.

Just unlock your phone, click the 3 dots in the top right corner of your screen and hit the "Rate and Review" button.
Enter your star rating and that's it! That's all you need to do.
I'll give you another 10 seconds just to finish sharing your thoughts.
----- Wait 10 seconds -----
Thank you so much for taking the time to leave a short review on Audible.
I am very appreciative as your review truly makes a difference for me.

Now back to your scheduled programming.

Fifteen Signs You're An Individualist

1. You need a lot of time alone to recharge.

2. You may be an artist – not just a visual artist but perhaps also a dancer, a writer or a musician.

3. You have a tendency to feel melancholy and may get depressed when times get rough.

4. You sometimes feel haunted by the thought that something is missing from your life and this contributes to a deep sense of longing.

5. Authenticity is all important to you, both in your work and in your relationships.

6. You view yourself as being fundamentally different to other people.

7. You are likely to be brutally honest and do not tend to hide your true feelings or motivations from yourself or from others.

8. You are willing to reveal things about yourself that most would never reveal for fear of being embarrassed or ashamed.

9. You have a deep yearning to connect with other people and you tend to feel misunderstood.

10. You've had more than one person in your life tell you that you're 'complicated' or 'weird.'

11. You suffer from low self-esteem and sometimes feel very alone in the world.

12. You are a highly sensitive person, and you have a hard time letting go of past hurts.

13. You'd rather have one close friendship than a hundred superficial ones.

14. Others sometimes accuse you of being moody.

15. Artist or not, you love to surround yourself with art and beautiful things.

Are lots of alarm bells going off in your head right now?

The Individualist Overview

Type Four on the Enneagram likes to think of him or herself as different or unique, indeed basing their very identity on such uniqueness. Feeling different is a double-edged sword to this type. On the one hand, it can cause them to feel special and superior and on the other, isolated and alone.

The Individualist will often be drawn to the arts. They might make a career in this area, becoming dancers, writers, visual artists, musicians or sculptors, for instance. Or maybe they will work closely with artists, perhaps managing museums or galleries or bringing arts to education. Or perhaps they will express this aspect of themselves in the way that they dress or present themselves, or simply in the idiosyncratic lifestyles that they lead.

The sensitivity of this type is heightened and they are emotionally complex souls. Authenticity is all important to the Achiever and he or she longs to be appreciated for his or her own authentic self. This type has no capacity for or interest in shallow relationships. They often feel unappreciated or misunderstood by others and, in these circumstances, will tend to withdraw from the world.

The inner life of the Four is rich and they will spend a lot of time immersed in their own internal world. This activity is important to them and will help them to process their inner feelings. Sometimes, they can express their inner lives in artistic ways. But it is important that they guard against withdrawing from real life completely.

Fours can be haunted by the notion that something fundamental is missing from their lives and this leaves them with a sense of longing, which can morph into melancholy. In times of great stress, this can develop into full blown depression. Self-absorption to an unhealthy level is a trap they can fall into.

It is important for the Individualist/Romantic to strive to be their own savior instead of looking to others to rescue them. They must learn to stand on their own two feet. Be your own rescue, number Four!

Examples of luminaries throughout history who have been Type Fours include: Rumi, Tchaikovsky, Anne Frank, Frida Kahlo, Rudolf Nureyov, Joni Mitchell, Leonard Cohen, Jackie Kennedy Onassis, Chopin, Gustav Mahler, Edgar Allen Poe, Virginia Wolfe, Anais Nin, Anne Rice, Martha Graham, Hank Williams, J.D. Salinger, Tennessee Williams, Billie Holiday, Cher, Alanis Morrisetter, Florence Welch, from Florence and The Machine, Stevie Nicks, Judy Garland, Cat Stevens, Annie Lennox, Amy WInehouse, Johnny Depp, Nicholas Cage, Angelina Jolie, Marlon Brando, Jeremy Irons, Prince, Kate Winslet and Winona Ryder.

The Individualist Levels

Healthy
Creativity

At his or her best, the healthy Individualist is a profoundly creative being. This creative stream flows strongly and freely, as they express their own personal feelings while at the same time inspiring others to connect with their own creativity and maybe even bring it to new levels. The healthy Four understands that what is personal is universal. She can transform any pain she might have experienced into gold, inspiring others in the process. This constant flow of creativity will enable the Individualist to self-renew and self-generate.

Self-Awareness
The Four's innate tendency for self-reflection leads to a deep understanding of the self that they can also use for the service of others, helping them to understand their feelings and motivations also. They are intuitive, in touch with their inner impulses and sensitive to the extreme, but in a positive way. They help and deal with other people in a compassionate, tactful and gentle way.

Individualism
The clue is in the name! Here, the Four's strong sense of individualism is expressed in a healthy way. The Four at this stage of their development knows him or herself extremely well and is always true to this self. The Type Four at this level is emotionally honest to a fault and has no problem revealing his or her true self, due to the knowledge that the whole range of emotions is common to all. They understand that the courage to show and express vulnerability is actually a strength. Deeply humane, these people can be surprisingly funny, possessing a very ironic view of life. Those around them come to rely on their emotional strength.

Neutral
Romanticism
The Four at this level of maturity strives to create an aesthetically beautiful life for him or herself. This is because a gorgeous environment uplifts them and elevates their mood. This could manifest in a beautiful home with original artwork adorning the walls. Although the Four is not completely immune to image-consciousness, he or she

is most concerned with choosing visual art that speaks to his or her soul. The Individualist or the Romantic at this level has a rich fantasy life and places a high value on passion and the imagination.

Self-Absorption
At a somewhat lower level, the tendency of Fours is to disappear too deeply into their own heads. They will internalize everything, becoming unhealthily introverted and overly moody. Here, the Individualist will be self-conscious and shy and will withdraw instead of dealing with their issues and bravely facing the world. They are hypersensitive and will go to great lengths to protect their self-image - essentially staying away from other people, whom they fear might too easily damage it.

Self-Pity
This tendency to go deeply within can descend into the Four living in a kind of fantasy world where they develop a sense of disdain for themselves and others. They can use this as an excuse to be self-indulgent in their emotions and habits and consequently go on to lead decadent and overly sensual lives. A healthy inclination towards daydreaming gets out of hand and they become increasingly unproductive and impractical. The Four might be envious of others at this level of maturity and this makes them even more melancholy.

Unhealthy
Alienation
Unhealthy fours experience alienation from both the self and others. Maybe they have been disappointed by dreams that have not come to fruition or people who have let them down. They will be very angry with themselves and this anger can turn inward and become depression. They feel blocked, both emotionally and creatively and this can expand into a feeling of paralysis. The sense of shame can be deep and all these negative emotions can leave the Four so exhausted that they can barely function.

Self-Contempt
The deeply unhealthy Four treats his or herself with contempt and believes absolutely that this is how other people view them too. They are tormented by desperate thoughts about their failings which sadly lead to feelings of self-hatred. The propensity to blame other people for all this pain results in the Four rejecting anyone who tries to help them.

Despair
A sense of hopelessness abounds and leads to self-destructive thoughts and behavior such as alcohol and drug abuse. Escaping profound pain is the aim here. At its absolute worst, the plight of the unhealthy Four is psychological breakdown or even suicide.

The Individualist Wings

Type Four with a Three Wing (4W3)
Think creativity, curiosity and a lively intelligence. This variant of the Type Three personality has a multitude of ideas and knows how to use them. The rich fantasy life of the Four is married with the drive and capacity for action of the Three, resulting in dreams becoming reality and creative businesses that thrive.

The practicality of the Three balances out the Four's proclivity for drama and melancholy. The focus is very much on career and ambitious goals. The Three wing can give the Four more confidence and extroversion. It can draw the normally introverted Four into more social settings and they might actually be able to enjoy group activities! The Three also lends energy which leads the Fours out of their heads and into the world.

The flip side of this, when the negative aspects of the Four combine with the negative aspects of the Three, is a different story. Then this variant will struggle with shame. They will become obsessive about the image they are projecting and their relationships will be filled with every kind of drama. They may look for a sense of authenticity outside of themselves - where it never is. They will try all sorts of tactics to seek approval, growing angry and competitive in the process. They might even get into financial difficulties as they spend excessively in an effort to impress.

Type Four With a Five Wing (4W5)
The healthy strain of this fusion results in a wonderful blend of the heart and the mind. The Four's inclination to delve deeply into feelings is tempered by the Five's impartiality. This can allow the Individualist to view his or her life in a more objective way - facts are more likely to be brought into play. In addition, the Four's depth of feeling merged with the Five's brain energy creates someone who is both wise and empathetic.

The intellectual capacity of the Five wonderfully complements the profound insight of the Individualist. The Four with a Five wing is a deep, sensitive and perceptive in often ground-breaking ways. They are often quiet and introverted on the outside but there is a lot of activity going on within - both intellectually and emotionally.

When the mix doesn't go so well, the Four with a Five wing can become overwhelmed by out-of-control thoughts and emotions. Their inner life becomes so intense that it is almost unbearable for them. When sufficiently tortured, the 4W5 will withdraw from the world, including from those close to them, feeling painfully alone. Their relationships could suffer and so could their careers. Their inner world becomes their reality and they will reject all offers of help, because they find it hard to trust. They feel that the weight of the world is on their shoulders and can find it a challenge to even look after their own basic needs.

Advice for The individualist

1. Order and discipline are not your natural enemies, especially when they are self-imposed. As a Type Four, you need a healthy dose of discipline to bring your inspired ideas out into the world, for instance, as artistic products or heart-centered businesses. Daydreaming will only get you so far. The world needs dreamers who make their dreams a reality!

2. Guard against your tendency towards self-indulgence, for example, when it comes to food, alcohol or drugs. You can help yourself by striving to maintain balance in your life, fostering healthy habits such as regular sleep, exercise and good nutrition.

3. Do not be a slave to your negative thought patterns. It is all too easy for Fours under stress to fall victim to the demons in their own heads. Find ways to distract yourself when you find yourself heading down a negative path - a favourite comedy show, uplifting music or a walk in the beauty of nature are just some examples. Just don't let yourself go down this route. It is the equivalent of beating yourself up.

4. You are not your feelings. Feelings are of the moment. They are not fixed and they do not define your character - they are not who you are. There is no need to let them lead you astray as they can be very misleading.

5. Don't wait until you are ready to try something or do something. You might never feel ready - a Four seldom will! The trick is to do it scared. To plough on regardless, even if all the pieces do not yet appear to be in place. There is real power in making a start and you will be amazed at how things come together as you go. Just do it!

Chapter Six - The Investigator (Type 5)

Also known as the Observer or the Sage

Fifteen Signs You're An Investigator

1. You have an insatiable need to find out why things are the way they are - scientifically and otherwise.

2. You have a strong urge to question the status quo.

3. You feel that a day in which you haven't learned anything new is a day wasted.

4. If a subject or activity captures your interest, you focus your attention on it intently, until you have fully mastered it.

5. You might have been described by others - either to your face or otherwise! - as eccentric.

6. You hate being pressured into making quick decisions.

7. You are inclined to hold tension in your gut.

8. You might sometimes feel that you are "stuck" in your head and that it takes quite an effort to get back into your body.

9. You are not big on small talk. You find it uncomfortable and, quite frankly, a complete waste of time.

10. Your privacy is of the utmost importance to you and it is quite common for you to experience other people as intrusive.

11. You might feel the need to acquire knowledge and expertise in a bid to overcome deep-seated feelings of inadequacy and self-doubt.

12. You are highly likely to be an expert in your field and that field might be scholarly or highly technical.

13. You have a propensity to withdraw into the safety of your mind when life seems too threatening or overly demanding.

14. You are most probably well-read, not to mention thoughtful and intelligent.

15. It takes you a while to become comfortable with another person, but once you have achieved that level of comfort, you are a devoted companion and that friendship is likely to last a lifetime.

Do you think you might possibly be a Five?

The Inspector Overview

The Investigator spends a lot of time in his or her own head. This is a similarity they have with the Four, but while the Four's comfort zone is in the realm of the imagination and the emotions, the five exists comfortably in the intellect. The Inspector has the habit of retreating into the world of thought when life gets too much. This is their safe place, where they can prepare to face the outside world once again because they like to be prepared and absolutely hate to be put on the spot. They are afraid, in fact, that they don't have what it takes to fully face life.

The Investigator, as the name implies, is sometimes scientifically oriented, but they may also strive for excellence in the area of the humanities.

The type Five can come across as eccentric. This might have something to do with their refusal to bend their beliefs to conform to the mainstream opinion. Freedom of thought is of paramount importance to the Observer, but they can be shy and struggle when it comes to dealing with and expressing their emotions. For this reason, relationships can be difficult for the type Five. This will make them feel lonely at times. Their independent nature can also add to the challenge of relationships, both in the romantic sense, but also when it comes to accepting help from well-meaning people.

The Investigator can be quite a sensitive soul. This makes them feel vulnerable so they commonly adopt coping mechanisms to shield themselves. This can make them come across as intellectually arrogant or carelessly indifferent. This also doesn't help with relationships! But if you learn how to penetrate these barriers, you've got yourself a friend for life.

Because of their need for privacy and fear of intrusion, Fives usually disguise their very strong feelings. This disguise can be extremely effective. For some Fives, one of their biggest fears is of being overwhelmed, so they attempt to keep their lives as simple as possible, making few demands on others in the hope that they will have few demands made on them in return.

Historical or famous Fives of note include: Albert Einstein, Stephen Hawking, Vincent Van Gogh, Georgia O'Keefe, Emily Dickinson, Bill Gates, Eckhart Tolle, Alfred Hitchcock, The Buddha, Oliver Sacks, Edvard Munch, Friedrich Nietzsche, James Joyce, Jean-Paul Sartre, Stephen King, Salvador Dali, Agatha Christie, Mark Zuckerberg, Kurt Kobain, Peter Gabriel, Marlene Dietrich, Jodie Foster, Gary Larson, David Lynch, Tim Burton, Stanely Kubrick, Annie Liebovitz and Susan Sontag.

The Investigator Levels

Healthy
Visionary
The healthy Five is open-minded to the core. He or she can see the big picture while at the same time, appreciating and comprehending the minutiae. Their view of the world is visionary, seeing everything that

can be improved for future generations and having some idea of how to make these improvements happen. They are the pioneers of the world; they are the scientists that make ground-breaking discoveries and the intellectuals that change the way we perceive the forces around us.

Observant
The healthy Five doesn't miss a thing. Their mental alertness is extraordinarily acute and their ability to focus and concentrate is second to none. They are perceptive and insightful with limitless curiosity. Their intellect is always seeking something new to sink its teeth into.

Expert
You will often find a five at the zenith of their chosen filed, as they have a seemingly unlimited capacity to attain mastery of whatever it is that interests them. They find knowledge wildly exciting and their passion often causes them to innovate and invent. Their work is often highly original and of great value to the world. The Investigator at this healthy level is frequently independent and possesses some marvellous idiosyncrasies.

Neutral
Conceptualizing
The Five will usually work everything out in their minds before acting on an idea. This allows them to fine tune everything from the outset. They love to be prepared and have all the required resources at their fingertips. They are studious and hard-working and often become specialists within their fields, while not being afraid to challenge the accepted way of doing things.

Detached
The Investigator, or the Observer, can sometimes become so involved in their intellectual world or the complex project on which they are

working, that they become quite detached from reality. They lose touch with the real world, often in quite a disembodied way and become so preoccupied by their visions that matters such as relationships go by the wayside. At this point, the Five displays a kind of high-strung intensity and might even develop a fascination with offbeat or disturbing subjects.

Antagonistic
Beware of trying to interfere with the not-so-mature Five's interior world. They will not thank you for it! They will defend their personal vision at all costs, becoming aggressive and rude with those who oppose their - often radical - views.

Unhealthy
Reclusive
The shyness of an unhealthy Five can go into overdrive. Not only do they become isolated from other humans, but also from reality. Their eccentricity is no longer pleasant and their personality becomes increasingly unstable. They shun company and tend to live a hermit-like existence.

Obsessive
This is obsession in its most unhealthy form. Their ideas become threatening - even to themselves. The Investigator in this state is delusional and suffers from phobias.

Deranged
At the lowest possible level, we are in the area of schizotypal personality disorders. It is a dangerously self-destructive state and psychosis or suicide may be the end result.

The Investigator Wings

Type Five with a Four wing (5W4)

The influence of the Four wing on the Type Five personality can cause them to be more comfortable when it comes to expressing their emotions. They are still curious, reserved and perhaps a little more creative.

It should come as no surprise that the Type Five with a Four wing likes to be alone as both types in their purity enjoy alone time.

The strengths of the 5W4 include a capacity for deep attentiveness and the ability to observe and understand the most tiny details. They think and express themselves creatively and work well independently. But like everyone else, The Type Five with a Four wing is by no means perfect. He or she can be hyper-sensitive and also struggle, at times, to think in a practical and realistic way. They can be too self-absorbed and are prone to distancing themselves from other people.

If you need to communicate with an Investigator with a Five wing, you will do well to be as clear as possible and give them adequate time to process before pressing them for a response. If you are working with them, you would be advised to keep meetings to a minimum, be concise in your explanations and sensitive when giving feedback.

This variant of the Observer is energized by gaining knowledge, new skills and by being appreciated. They will feel drained if they have to spend too much time with other people or forced into situations that overwhelm them. And they certainly do not appreciate harsh criticism!

Type Five with a Six wing (5W6)

When the Six wing is dominant in the Type Five, the Investigator becomes more cooperative. Such a person will also be more inclined to use their impressive knowledge to solve problems rather than to intellectualize. This modification on the Five is inclined to be logical, independent and practical. They desire to be of use and to put their knowledge to work. They want to make the world a better place and feel more worthy in the process.

Their more positive traits include such qualities as focus and good organization, not to mention a passion for learning and improving. They often have a great capacity for solving complex problems and they are the type you want to have around in a crisis as they are adept at remaining calm.

However, the Type Five with a Six wing does have various blind spots. They can have difficulty relating to others and can be overly defensive in their wish to protect their privacy. They can come across as cold and aloof and need to be inspired in order to take any action.

This alternative Investigator loves to solve problems, especially when it makes them feel as if they are making a valuable contribution to society. Their pursuit of knowledge is enthusiastic, particularly when it comes to areas in which they are personally interested. They are drained by spending too much time around others and energized by spending time alone. Always be aware of their propensity for self-doubt in your dealings with them.

Advice for The Investigator

1. Stay in your body. Your intellect is a wonderful tool but it is also necessary to stay connected to other people and to the real world. An excellent way of doing this is by staying in touch with your body and your physical sensations through exercise.

2. Trust is an issue for a Five and because of this, they can find it very hard to open up to other people. When they experience conflict in a relationship, their natural tendency is to withdraw and isolate themselves. This is, of course, not particularly healthy behavior. The Investigator would do well to remember that conflicts are a normal part of every relationship and the appropriate course of action is to work things out.

3. It is tough for Type Five on The Enneagram to relax. This is because of their innate intensity. It is therefore important for the Five to devise ways to wind down that are suitable and appropriate. Meditation, yoga and running are all recommended.

4. The Five can lose his or her sense of perspective and quite easily feel overwhelmed as there are so many factors to consider! To help you make an accurate assessment in these circumstances, seek out the advice of someone you trust (after first working on your trust issues)!

5. Be selective in the projects you choose to become involved with. Make sure that they are life-affirming and take you in the direction in which you want to go. Make sure you are not distracting yourself in an unworthy way and wasting your precious time.

Chapter Seven - The Loyalist (Type 6)

Also known as the Loyal Skeptic or the Traditionalist

Fifteen Signs You're A Loyalist

1. You hang on to toxic friendships and situations longer than you should.

2. You are perceived - and quite rightly so - as a good trouble-shooter. This is because you are excellent at anticipating problems and devising appropriate solutions.

3. You can hold a lot of tension in the area around your diaphragm.

4. You worry a lot. Let's face it, there are so many things that can go wrong!

5. You are loyal to ideas and belief systems as well as to your friends and family members.

6. You can have trouble connecting with your own inner guidance system. This can cause you to lack confidence in your own judgment.

7. A sense of security is of the utmost importance to you and finding and holding on to this security is a driving force.

8. You tend to ask for advice from many different people before making a decision. As you mature, however, the amount of people upon whose opinion you rely may lessen.

9. You are contradictory in nature and your personality contains many opposites. This is because you tend to go back and forth

between various different influences. To paraphrase Walt Whitman - you are large, you contain multitudes!

10. The people around you know that you are reliable and that they can depend on you. You are always there for them.

11. You appreciate order. It is important for you to have a firm structure in place, to have double-checked all your facts and to have a back-up plan.

12. Peace of mind can be elusive for you.

13. You can be suspicious of other people and authorities. You wait until the person or organization has proven themselves fully before giving them your trust.

14. You might have a tendency to act defiantly against whatever it is that you find threatening. In this instance, you may become a rebel and challenge authority.

15. You are responsible, hard-working and trustworthy. Those who are lucky enough to have your friendship know that you will always have their backs.

Did you say "that could be me" more than a few times? If so, read on. You could be a Loyalist!

The Loyalist Overview

As a typical Six, you crave security above all else. This is because you wrestle with a deep-rooted sense of anxiety which is at the core of your being, whether you are aware of it or not.
Type Six on The Enneagram tends to worry a lot. They have no problem imagining all sorts of scenarios, far-fetched or otherwise, in which everything goes wrong. They fear that there is nothing steady

enough to hold on to, so they attempt to create such steadiness for themselves, often in personal relationships.

Their propensity to imagine every single possible disastrous outcome makes the Type Six an excellent trouble-shooter, and therefore very useful for others to have around. But this is not much of a comfort for the Loyalist, who struggles to find peace of mind with this constant focus on potential problems.

This can also have the effect of causing the Six to lack spontaneity. Because how can they possibly carry out an action without meticulous planning first? If they don't do this, won't everything collapse like a house of cards?

This is a lot of anxiety to live with. It also makes the Six more suspicious than the average person. You really have to prove yourself to win the Loyalist's trust. But once you succeed in doing so, you have a steadfast friend for life. Loyalty is a fantastic trait, but the Six would do well to make sure they are not staying loyal to someone or something long after it is time to move on from them.

The Six often has a complicated relationship with authority. On the one hand, their desire to have someone or something to believe in might cause them to give their control over to an external force. On the other hand, they also have the propensity to distrust and be suspicious of authority. How confusing! Sometimes a Six individual will lean further in one direction than the other. Sometimes, they might go back and forth between these two different attitudes.

The Loyalist also has two different strategies when it comes to coping with fear. One strategy is phobic, which will cause them to be compliant and cooperative. The other is counter-phobic, which means that the Six will take a defiant stand against anything they find threatening. Rebelliousness and aggression can be the hallmark here.

There have been countless noteworthy Loyalists. Here are a number of them: Sigmund Freud, Robert F. Kennedy, Malcolm X, Diana, Princess of Wales, U2's Bono, Julia Roberts, Ellen Degeneres, Spike Lee, Krishnamurti, Edgar Hoover, George H.W. Bush, J.R.R. Tolkein,

Melissa Etheridge, Bruce Springsteen, Mike Tyson, Woody Allen, Sally Field, David Letterman, Newt Gingrich, Jay Leno, Katie Holmes, Benn Affleck, Tom Hanks, Mel Gibson, Diane Keaton, Mark Wahlberg, Dustin Hoffman, Oliver Stone, Michael Moore, John Grisham, Prince Harry, Robert F. Kennedy, Mark Twain and Richard Nixon.

The Loyalist Levels

Healthy
Trusting
This trust is for the self yet it also extends to others. The healthy Six has got the balance right, maintaining their independence while at the same time achieving a cooperative interdependence with others. They are able to collaborate with others and work together in harmony. When the Six learns to believe in herself, she can act with courage and positivity, making her a fabulous leader. She will also be richly self-expressive.

Appealing to Others
When the Six is fully mature and gets her or himself together, they can be a most endearing and lovable type. People react strongly to them in a very positive way and have a genuine affection for them, which they are likely to receive back in kind. Once they have their trust issues sorted out, the healthy Six successfully blends with others, leading to fruitful friendships and alliances.

Dedicated
When the healthy Loyalist finds a movement or an individual in which they fully believe, there is no one who is more dedicated. They will build communities, sacrifice for others or for a greater cause, and bring

cooperation, security and stability wherever they go. They are determined, reliable, trustworthy and responsible.

Neutral
Safe
At this neutral level, a kind of contraction occurs and the Loyalist has more of a tendency to play it safe. This is not always a terrible thing. At this point of their development, the Six invests their energy in whatever seems likely to remain stable and secure. They organize and create structure and look to authorities that can promise a sense of continuity. They never let up in anticipating what can go wrong and trying to put systems in place to prevent such problems occurring.

Indecisive
If the Six in neutral mode feels confused or that too many demands are being made on him or her, they will give off many contradictory signals. They will procrastinate and become overly cautious, indecisive and evasive. They will be increasingly negative as their anxiety levels rise and unpredictability results. They may even react in passive-aggressive ways.

Reactive
The fear takes over the Six, although they may not consciously be aware of this. Instead, they blame other people for their uncomfortable feelings, taking it out on the "outsider," for instance. They will be defensive at this level and highly sensitive to threats, constantly monitoring others to work out whether they are a friend or foe. They can be authoritarian and suspicious of everyone and their manner can become belligerent.

Unhealthy
Panicked
Fear takes over at this unhealthy stage. This highly insecure feeling causes the Six to panic and become extremely volatile. They look for

increasingly strong authority figures and institutions in order to buoy up their own acute feelings of inferiority and defenselessness. They will be extremely critical and difficult to be around.

Persecuted
This all-pervasive feeling that others are out to get them can make the unhealthy Six lash out irrationally which, in the worst case scenario, can lead to violence.

Hysterical
This is the lowest a Six can go. It is a self-destructive level where alcohol and drugs might be abused. It is the realm of the Paranoid Personality Disorders and they might even attempt to take their own lives.

The Loyalist Wings

Type Six with a Five wing (6W5)
For the most part, the Type Six with a Five wing is a traditional sort, conservative in their views and desirous of fitting into a trustworthy group. Safety is the name of the game here. Although the Six desire to feel secure is colored by the Five need to analyze things right down to their component parts.

When well-balanced, the 6W5 is able to let go of anxiety. This makes them good-humored, relaxed and endearing. They finally feel that they can trust life and in turn, this is a person that can be trusted and relied upon one-hundred-percent.

It is lovely to have the balanced Type Six with a Five wing as a family member. Possessing a quiet confidence, they will be a wonderful companion and source of wisdom. You will be able to develop a deep bond with this type and the Five wing will add a perceptiveness to their enduring friendship.

But imbalance can sometimes ensue and anxiety can rear its ugly head again. They look for a reason for this rising tension and if one is not easily forthcoming, they will find someone to blame for it!

If stress levels increase, the world becomes an increasingly threatening place for the 6W5 and paranoia can begin to set in. They might feel that everybody is out to get them and in this desperately uncomfortable place of tension, they might look for somebody to come to their rescue. Sixes want to be likable and attractive to others, but Five does not really know how to achieve this. Their attire tends not to be overly showy or flashy.

It may suit the Loyalist with a Five wing to find employment that combines being part of a group with being alone. A forest ranger or a bus driver might be an example of this. Some become involved in risky protection activities such as fire-fighting and others might look for ways to advocate for under privileged people.

The Type Six with a Seven wing (6W7)

The Type Six with a Seven wing is a lot less subdued than the Type Six with a Five wing. Their reactions are more impulsive and colourful and they are less likely to analyze a situation, instead jumping in with both feet. However, the caution of the Six will usually pull back the flamboyance of the Seven before it gets too out-of-hand.

There is a back and forth here between flamboyance and caution which can cause some emotional volatility.

At its best, the Loyalist with a Seven wing is steady, calm and deliberate. When in balance, both the Six's anxiety and the Seven's impulsiveness tend to diminish. They still love having fun with their friends but the desperate drive for security is transformed into an inner strength. They make great parents or siblings.

The 6W7 frequently develops a strong spiritual side, experiencing a deep sense of belonging with the universe. Their faith is a great source of comfort to them.

Of course, things can get out of kilter. If the Type Six with a Seven wing gets out of whack, anxiety and insecurity come to the fore once more. Here, they will jump from one extreme emotional state to the other, desperately searching for someone to help them and feeling increasing despair.

In a more stressed state, the 6W7 can come across as clingy and desperate and this drives other people away. They get themselves into all sorts of trouble as they feel increasingly dependent and tense.

This variant of the Six is often physically attractive and appealing to the opposite sex. In terms of the world of work, they may look to fun professions which also have an element of security inherent in them such as cartoonists or movie reviewers.

Advice for The Loyalist

1. Trust is an issue for you. If you are honest with yourself, you can most probably identify a few people in your life that you can trust completely. Cherish these people and hold them dear. Let them know how much you appreciate them, even though this might make you feel vulnerable. If you genuinely do not have anyone in your life that you feel you can trust, make it a point to find someone, believing that there are trustworthy people out there. You may have to move past your fears to do so, but the end result will be worth it.

2. The Type Six can sometimes use projection as a defense mechanism, in other words, attributing to others what you cannot accept in yourself. This hardly seems fair, does it? Watch out for your tendency to resort to this behaviour. Do not blame others for things that you yourself have done or brought upon yourself in some way. You become your own worst enemy when you become negative and self-doubting, causing even more harm to yourself than you do to others.

3. Do all you can to quell your anxiety. A key step might be to just accept that this is part of your nature and also to acknowledge

that more people suffer from anxiety than you probably realize. Try to relax. Everything is going to be fine!

4. Other people like you more than you think they do. That's something else to stop worrying about!

5. Try not to overreact when you are under stress. This involves managing your own thoughts more effectively and acknowledging that most of what you have wasted your time worrying about has never arisen. Fearful thoughts have no purpose but to weaken your ability to act and make things better.

Chapter Eight - The Enthusiast (Type 7)

Also known as the Epicure

Fifteen Signs You're an Enthusiast

1. You are very curious and always looking for new experiences to prevent boredom from creeping in!

2. You are wonderfully optimistic and enthusiastic, something other people often find "catching" and love to be around.

3. You don't store as much tension in your body as other types and tend to be loose and flexible. The challenge for you is to stay grounded.

4. You are not really concerned with the image you project and are more interested in having fun and doing your own thing.

5. Other people accuse you of being restless and may comment that you have trouble settling down to one thing.

6. You see life as an exciting adventure, with something better always around the corner.

7. You are probably an extrovert and great at networking.

8. You don't believe in denying yourself anything - you want to experience all the pleasures that life has to offer.

9. You seek distraction from internal negativity in the external world, for example, by keeping really busy and making sure you are stimulated at all times.

10. You have above average or high self-esteem, believing in your strengths and your talents.

11. You are versatile and can often be multi-talented. Highly practical, you can be engaged in many projects at once.

12. You are most probably intelligent with an agile mind, but not necessarily studious or intellectual.

13. You may have brilliant mind-body co-ordination and manual dexterity.

14. You are naturally good-humored and cheerful, and normally do not take yourself too seriously.

15. You have an over-arching desire to live life to the fullest!

Did you recognize yourself in the above signs? Were you proud? Read on and find out if this is your Type.

The Enthusiast Overview

As far as the Enthusiast is concerned, life is meant to be one big, exciting adventure from start to finish. This makes them fun to be around and people are naturally attracted to their *joie de vivre*. They are always looking to the future and looking forward to something better that's around the next corner.

Most Sevens are extroverted. They have tons of energy which they like to expend in all sorts of ways, being multi-talented and creative. Indeed, they are highly practical with multiple skills and may possess an entrepreneurial spirit. If they do have a flaw in this regard, it is that they sometimes have difficulty focusing. Also, they have so many interests and such high hopes for the "next big thing" that they can find it hard to settle on just one project and bring it fully to fruition. They will, however, be adept at promoting themselves and their product, business or service and they are natural networkers.

Sevens do not believe in denying themselves and they can be compulsive pleasure seekers. They sometimes use this activity to distract themselves from anything negative that might be going on in their lives. This may lead to a tendency towards addiction - drugs, gambling, etc.

The typical Enthusiast, or Epicure, as he or she is also known, is usually not lacking in confidence. While this is healthy, this can at times veer towards being self-centered or having an inflated sense of entitlement.

The Seven does not always like confronting the harsh realities of life and other people's problems, but if they run away from confronting such emotions, they run the risk of storing up problems for themselves and suffering from anxiety or depression down the road.

Of course, there have been loads of famous Sevens. Some you have most probably heard of are: The Dalai Lama, Mozart, John F. Kennedy, Richard Branson, Bette Midler, Goldie Hawn, Robin Williams, Galileo Galilei, Thomas Jefferson, Amelia Earhart, Kandinsky, Noel Coward, Joe Biden, Silvio Berlusconi, Suze Orman, Elton John, Fred Astaire, Joan Rivers, George Clooney, Jim Carrey, Leonardo DiCaprio, Cameron Diaz, Simon Cowell, Larry King, Howard Stern, David Duchovny, Robert Downey Junior, Brad Pitt, Cary Grant, Stephen Spielberg, Russell Brand, Miley Cyrus, Sacha Baron Cohen and Sarah Palin.

The Enthusiast Levels

Healthy
Joyful
The Enthusiast at his highest level is all gratitude and appreciation for everything he has, including all the simple pleasures in life. This

ability to assimilate experiences in an in-depth way leads to a kind of ecstasy that borders on the spiritual.

Enthusiastic
Well, it is their name! This extroverted type is good-humored, lively and spontaneous. They respond to everything in an excitable and eager way, finding even "normal" life experiences quite invigorating.

Multi-talented
Their many gifts make them accomplished and productive - well able to achieve in lots of different areas. Due to their enthusiasm for a broad range of subjects, they can often be compelled to develop a variety of skills.

Neutral
Restless
So many choices, so little time - this could be the mantra of the average Enthusiast. They have a fear of missing out which makes it difficult for them to choose between one option and another. Focus can be difficult to achieve as they are constantly seeking out new adventures. They can be sophisticates at this stage in their maturity. They like variety, plenty of cash and keeping up with the latest fashion.

Hyperactive
The fear of being bored keeps the Seven at this level in constant motion. They don't know what they need to feel satisfied so they throw themselves into perpetual activity. They will perform and exaggerate and behave in more and more flamboyant ways. They will find it difficult to follow through on their ideas.

Consuming
They never feel that they have enough. They consume to excess, whether that be shopping, food or drugs. They are never satisfied, no matter what, and this can lead them to be demanding and hardened.

Unhealthy
Addicted
The unhealthy Seven does not know when to stop. They cannot control their impulses and so desperate are they to soothe their anxiety. They can sink to levels of depravity and their behavior may become abusive and offensive.

Out of Control
From bad to worse! In a desperate bid for escapism, these Sevens are incapable of dealing with anxiety properly and may descend into erratic or impulsive actions.

Self-Destructive
The lowest possible level for the Seven to sink to. They have probably ruined their health at this point and given up on themselves and life. They're most likely deeply depressed and may attempt suicide. Their symptoms here would not be dissimilar to bipolar disorder.

The Enthusiast Wings

The Seven with a Six wing (7W6)
The hallmarks of a Seven with a Six wing are that they are enthusiastic and adventurous - as you would expect with a seven - but with a healthy dose of responsibility thrown into the mix. Sounds like quite a good balance, doesn't it? They still love to pursue new experiences but they are much better able to stick to prior commitments.

Although this all sound perfect, there is a potential downside too: a Fear of Missing Out (FOMO)! The Seven with a Six wing really wants to honor their commitments, but what if a wonderful last minute opportunity arises? You can see how this variant of the number Seven is likely to feel torn. They want, most of all, to feel happy and fulfilled and the way the Seven goes about this is by finding joy in even the smallest of experiences. But the Seven with a Six wing might have a tendency to rationalize away negative feelings, unconsciously convincing themselves of their own happiness when this is, in fact, not the case.

They will go to great lengths to avoid being upset - even rationalizing and justifying the bad behavior of others, because they value happiness and optimism above all else. Relationships are very important to them, as is pleasure-seeking on all levels and this all abiding fear of missing out on potential opportunities.

The Enthusiast with a Six wing has many positive traits. The inclination is to be highly productive. They also cooperate well with others, whether they are fellow workers, clients or other collaborators. They manage to remain sensitive to the feelings of others, not riding roughshod over their emotions in the pursuit of their own goals and happiness. Even when confronted with a stressful situation, the Seven's optimism will pull them through and allow them to remain buoyant. They are quick thinkers but do not merely consider the surface issues. They are capable of going deep and considering matters in a thorough way.

But, of course, we all have our blind spots to contend with and this variant of the Type Seven is no exception to that rule. Unlike the "pure" Type Seven, the Seven with a Six wing cares deeply about what other people think of them and is easily affected by their opinions. This might cause them to doubt themselves and lead to a feeling of all-pervading anxiety. And the Seven's propensity to become bored does not go away. They may easily become restless in a job or a relationship and crave something new. And when stress hits, the Enthusiast with a Six wing could struggle with organization and focus.

When dealing with an Enthusiast with this wing, you will do well to remain optimistic and upbeat and to really listen to them, taking all their ideas seriously. They love to chat in a free-flowing, light-hearted way and they also greatly appreciate encouragement and support. This will especially be the case when they are expressing difficult emotions, which they find challenging.

Remember how much they are energized by new ideas and experiences and how creativity inspires them. They love meeting new people and going to places where there are large gatherings of folk to get to know. Take your 7W6 to a party or a concert. They will love you for it!

What they do not thrive on is overly rigid schedules or rules. Do not beat them down with negativity and make sure that the Seven with a Six wing in your life has plenty of company to keep them happy and energized. They absolutely hate routine and thrive on lots of interesting choices - not to mention the freedom to make such choices.

In summary, the Enthusiast with a Six wing is a curious type and can be wildly productive given the right circumstances. Although they still seek new experiences, they are steadfastly loyal to friends and family. Creative and adventurous, they also love to build a sense of community. They are sometimes known as "The Pathfinder."

Type Seven with an Eight wing (7W8)

The Eight wing lends a toughness to the Type Seven. It also inclines them to be more work-oriented. They are still enthusiastic - as the main hallmark of umber Seven on The Enneagram - but they have an added determination.

In a general sense, there is still a fear of missing out, but this manifests itself more in a fear of deprivation rather that a fear of missing out on excitement. The pursuit of new opportunities is still a high priority and so is the dislike of rigidity and scheduling. The Seven's basic desire to be happy and fulfilled is tempered somewhat by the Eight wing and can now be more accurately described as a wanting to be satisfied and content.

Although they still love to be out in the world, going to events where there are lots of people, such as big parties and festivals and also travelling to exotic places, the Eight wing gives a more protectionist dimension to the Seven's actions and they defend themselves by justifying the poor behavior of others and by rationalizing away their own bad feelings.

Optimism is still a top priority for the Seven with an Eight wing, as is personal gratification. They are always on the lookout for new opportunities and consider it highly important to be open to new experiences. Fear of missing out does not go away with the presence of the Eight wing. They still crave and adore the company of other humans and will justify the negative actions of such humans to prevent themselves from feeling bad.

This variant of the Seven wing has many attributes. They have a knack for remaining positive, no matter what, and staying in that all-important high energy mindset. Self-confidence comes to them easily and they often have a natural charisma that attracts other people like bees around a honey pot. They are no shrinking violets either, and are able to stand up for and assert themselves. They are a good sort to have around you in a crisis, as they have the ability to remain calm in situations where many people are in a panic.

Like everyone else, however, the Enthusiast with an Eight wing has weaknesses that they must strive to overcome. The Eight wing does make the all-encompassing charm of the number Seven slightly less pervasive. Because of this, the Seven with an Eight wing can come across as quite blunt at times. They may offend people without realizing or without meaning to do so. They can also be impatient with situations and people. The Enthusiast with an Eight wing might be accused of focusing too much on their career and to the detriment of other aspects of their lives such as their relationships. They might be overly materialistic also, forgetting what is truly important in life. In spite of all this, they could still suffer from the Type Seven tendency to have difficulty following through on plans, once the initial enthusiasm has worn off.

When you are communicating with this alternative to the Type Seven, they will really appreciate it if you listen carefully to them. This is because they love to have conversations and expressing themselves is very important to them. They like their conversations to have a purpose, not just to wander aimlessly and their preference is to keep things upbeat. They want to get right to the point while also having the opportunity to share every single thought and idea that is going on inside their heads. They appreciate people being direct and honest with them and will happily cooperate to reach a compromise if an argument arises.

If you have a Seven with an Eight wing in your life, never lose sight that they love new experiences, especially fun occasions such as parties and celebrations, concerts and festivals and travelling to new and far flung destinations. Relationships are a big priority for them and you will get on better with your 7W6 if you allow them to be the center of attention from time to time! And they dearly love a good goal to accomplish.

Do not cut off their energy with rigid rules and limits. They hate, above all, to feel controlled. They also thrive on company - so why not give them yours?

The Type Seven with an Eight wing is sometimes known as the Opportunist.

Advice for The Enthusiast

1. You love to have conversations and express all your many varied opinions, but be honest with yourself. Are you *really* listening to those with whom you are having conversations?

Active listening is an art worth cultivating. Think of all the new and interesting things you'll discover if you really take in what other people are saying to you. It might even lead to new opportunities. And there doesn't always have to be chatter. Silence is golden. Do not be afraid to put down your phone or turn off the TV. There are real and lasting benefits to be had from not distracting yourself all the time and staying present with your thoughts and emotions. Living with less external stimulation in this way, will help you to trust yourself. You might even be more satisfied when you start doing less. Now doesn't that sound like a huge relief?

2. Life is long and you don't have to experience everything all in one go. Imagine having every dinner you were ever going to eat all in one day! You would not want that. So that tempting car or cake, for instance, will still be in the show room or the shop next week – there may even be a better alternative. Let go of your compulsive fear of missing out on opportunities. They will come around again and you will be better able to judge which ones are really meant for you.

3. As a typical Seven, you would be well advised to observe your impulses instead of diving in head first. Do not give into them straight away, no matter how much you might want to do so. Instead, learn to judge which ones are worthy of acting upon. Not all impulses are created equally! As you become more observant and a better judge of all your different impulses, you will learn which ones are worth your focus, time and energy, and you can start living your life in a more beneficial way.

4. Experience is not all about quantity. It is about quality too. In other words, a few wonderful and deeply felt experiences can be better than a thousand scattered ones where you do not really allow yourself to be present. Good advice for the Seven is to stay in the moment and pay attention to what you are actually doing in the now, instead of constantly anticipating potentially better experiences. The latter is not the path to true satisfaction.

5. Question your desires. Is what you want really what you want? When you consider the likely long-term consequences of your current desires, do you still think you're longing for the right thing for you? Or will it only lead to disappointment or even unhappiness in the long run? Practice discernment at all times.

Chapter Nine - The Challenger (Type 8)

Also known as the Ruler

Fifteen Signs You're a Challenger

1. You like to be in charge. And why on earth *wouldn't* anyone put you in charge of things?

2. You hate, hate, hate to be controlled. In fact, you rarely let this happen to you and anyone who tries is met with a lot of attitude.

3. Others might accuse you of being domineering.

4. You have the capacity to work extremely hard in order to manifest your goals.

5. You are an excellent mentor and can effectively show others how to achieve as you have done, thus nurturing the leaders of the future.

6. You have a propensity for getting bored very quickly. This can also lead to impatience.

7. You can come across as somewhat fierce and others can find you intimidating at times.

8. Anger can be an issue for you and you are inclined to lose your temper fairly easily. Some people find this scary!

9. As the name of this type implies, you love to take on a challenge and indeed, enjoy giving other people challenges too, thereby helping them to stretch their abilities and even to exceed themselves.

10. You have an in-built charisma or magnetism. This makes you an effective leader, no matter what sphere you live and work in. You can quite easily persuade others to follow you.

11. You have great energy and you use this - together with your formidable willpower - to leave your mark on society

12. You value independence highly and you are not afraid to stand alone, defying social convention if necessary.

13. You possess a steely determination which others find amazing and sometimes even logic-defying.

14. You have a powerful 'can do' attitude and tend to be extremely resourceful. You get things done, in a commanding way.

15. You have an abundance of common sense and this can greatly benefit those around you.

So what do you think? Are you a Challenger? Other people can offer their opinions but only you know for sure.

The Challenger Overview

Control is at the heart of the Challenger's personality. At their core, they are totally unwilling to be controlled, whether it be by a person or by circumstances. It is of the utmost importance to an Eight that they remain the masters of their fates and the captains of their souls. The flip side of this is that they are inclined to be domineering. This coupled with their unwillingness to be controlled may lead them to try to control others. Ironic, is it not? A healthy Challenger is well able to keep this tendency under control but it is something that always has to be guarded against, especially as one moves down the maturity scale. It can be a recurring issue in the interpersonal relationships of an Eight.

Eights take the concept of being strong-willed to new heights. They are tough-minded to a fault and their enormous energy and practical nature aids them significantly in getting their own way.

The Challenger desires to get the most out of life and this can often extend to their physical appetites. They indulge in those appetites without experiencing a hint of unhealthy remorse.

Financial independence is a massive priority for the Challenger. He or she may have difficulty having a boss. They do know best, after all! Challengers tend to benefit from working in a field where they can be their own boss. Under certain circumstances, an Eight may feel the need to opt out of society altogether, finding other ways to gain financial freedom instead, as they are usually uncomfortable with hierarchies.

The Challenger has a deep and abiding fear of feeling vulnerable. This can be detrimental to their capacity to form intimate relationships because, obviously, intimacy requires vulnerability. Defenses need to be lowered! Of course, this involves letting go of the need to be in control and trust is of the greatest importance in this arena. Betrayal of any kind will cut the challenger to the quick. Woe betide the person who violates an Eight in this way!

Believe it or not, Eights can be sentimental. They hide it well, even from those closest to them, but it's true. This is an indication of how much the Eight fears being vulnerable. However, if you do manage to win their trust, you will have someone who stands by you no matter what. The Challenger is hugely protective of those in their inner circle - family and friends especially - and they will move mountains to provide for these people.

A big Achilles Heel for the Eight is their anger. At lower levels of maturity, this emotion can spiral out of control and turn into rage. Such aggression can even turn into violence and unhealthy Eights can be intimidating, ruthless and even dangerous.

Not surprisingly, there are many Eights who have achieved remarkable feats of success in this life. Some examples of these include: Winston Churchill, Oskar Schindler, Martin Luther King, Serena Williams,

Barbara Walters, Toni Morrison, Frank Sinatra, Bette Davis, Paul Newman, Richard Wagner, Franklin D. Roosevelt, Fidel Castro, Lyndon Johnson, Golda Meir, Saddam Hussein, Donald Trump, Ernest Hemingway, James Brown, Queen Latifah, Aretha Franklin, Pink, Jack Black, Sean Connery, John Wayne, Mae West, Humphrey Bogart, Jack Black, Dr Phil, Roseanne Barr, Jack Nicholson, Tommy Lee Jones, Clint Eastwood, Lauren Bacall, Chrissie Hynde, Courtney Love, Pablo Picasso, Norman Mailer, Senator John McCain and last but not least, Indira Gandhi.

The Challenger Levels

Healthy
Heroism
Not unlike Type One on the Enneagram, Type Eight possesses the qualities that heroes are made of. There is the potential here to climb awesome heights and to achieve historical greatness. At the peak of his or her health and maturity, an Eight can restrain their lesser impulses and become a truly magnanimous individual, attaining true self-mastery. Possessing massive courage, they are willing to face real danger in order to achieve their vision and make a true difference.

Strong
This strength comes with a remarkable self-confidence and self-assertiveness. They have no problem standing up for their needs and wants. The Eight at this healthy stage is full of drive and passion and no one is more resourceful than them. A 'can do' attitude is dominant in these types.

Authoritative
The natural leader or commander. The Eight will be the one who is not afraid to take the initiative to get things done and make things happen. Decision-making comes easily to them as they rarely doubt their own

judgment. They are the people's champion. They will provide and protect and carry those who lack their strength. They are truly honourable.

Neutral
Self-sufficient
It is of utmost importance to the Challenger, at this stage of their development, that they have adequate resources, financially and otherwise. To this end, they will become profoundly pragmatic and enterprising. They will be the quintessential 'wheeler-dealer,' willing to deny even their own emotional needs as they take any necessary risks and put their noses to the grindstone.

Domineering
At this not-so-mature level, the Challenger will seek to bend others' wills to their own. They have no compunction about imposing their vision on everyone else. Dominating other people, and equally their environment, the Eight will become a 'show off' and overly forceful. They do not appreciate anybody who has the temerity to question their word or their decisions and they must feel that people are supporting their efforts. They become egocentric at this point and forget to treat other individuals with the respect that they want and deserve.

Intimidating
Matters go from bad to worse - for Eights and those around them - as we travel further down the maturity ladder. This is where the Challenger becomes more than challenging - they become adversarial, belligerent and confrontational. They will refuse to back down, even if they secretly suspect that they are wrong. This would be tantamount to losing face and they cannot allow that to happen! They will threaten and impose punishments in order to extract obedience from those around them, who at this stage are feeling increasingly insecure. They are their own worst enemies however, as their attitude and actions may

well backfire, turning people against them and perhaps even causing them to join together against the Eight.

Unhealthy

Ruthless
At this immature level of development, things start to get quite nasty. Here the Eight will stop at nothing to get their own way including immoral behaviour and violence. If they are in a position to get away with being dictatorial, then they certainly will! They might resort to criminal behaviour, not caring if they rip people off. They will defy all attempts to control them.

Delusional
Oh dear! At this stage of bad emotional health, the Eight will think that he or she is invincible. Their antics will now border on megalomania and extreme recklessness will be the order of the day. They believe they are truly invulnerable.

Vengeful
"Never surrender!" will be their battle-cry, but not in a good way. At the lowest of the low, the Challenger will destroy everything and everyone that does not bend to their will. They will descend to all sorts of barbaric conduct, even murder. We are in the territory here of the sociopath.

The Challenger Wings

The Eight with a Seven wing (8W7)
A person doesn't get any tougher than the Type Eight with a Seven wing. They might even look tough, with broad, rough features and an enormous, muscular physique. And their actions might well match

their appearance. This is because the Challenger with a Seven wing has so much powerful energy coursing through their system. The Eight's overpowering personality tends to dominate quite a bit and values being in charge above all else, including the Seven's need to be the life and soul of the party.

Their mode of appearance can vary wildly. When they are in the mood and the circumstances are right, they might be very well dressed and 'pulled together.' But at other times, when they are preoccupied, they might not be bothered at all about what they look like.

Of course, every single personality has the capacity to shine and the Eight with a Seven wing is no exception to this. When they're well-balanced, an 8W7 can be charming and tactful. If they have a sense of self-awareness, this can make them less aggressive and less extreme in their conduct. They realize that real power comes from within and that they do not have to put on a show of strength. They discover patience and learn to calm their more destructive impulses.

At their peak, the Challenger with a Seven wing will choose kindness instead of being argumentative. Picture a gentle giant. They will use their power for good, becoming considerate and perceptive in their dealings with people. They get in touch with their intuition and this allows them to accurately judge various situations. The highly integrated 8W7 has options available to him or her which are not possible at a lower level.

But with the good comes the bad. The Challenger with a Seven wing can actually be a physical danger to others. Insensitive, unsociable, with no regard for the rules that govern a civilized society, the 8W7 becomes a very rough character indeed. Think, here, of the quintessential bully or thug.

With even less integration, this variant of the Eight will lash out violently. He or she will be judgmental, defensive and intolerant. Their mantra is 'kill or be killed.'

In terms of professions that suit this type of Eight, they may include things like construction foreman, army general, or boxer. Of course, they can also be a stay-at-home mother! It is all possible.

The Eight with a Nine wing (8W9)

Physical power is still a huge component when it comes to the Challenger with a Nine wing. But Type Nine on The Enneagram has a passive quality causing this particular personality to be quiet but aggressive when provoked. Imagine a bear, normally slow-moving but capable of sudden violence. Eruptions of anger are possible. They usually move around quite slowly but they must feel that the situation is under control before they can relax.

When well-balanced, this variant of the Eight is a joy to be around. They will be kind and gentle and in touch with their inner guidance. They will not feel the need to dominate. Neither will they feel an impulse to withdraw. They wield their power wisely, knowing when it is of benefit to themselves and others to do so, and sensing when it is not.

At the very top level, the 8W9 possesses a powerful benevolence and has the capacity to be a great leader or teacher. They are tough when it is needed and gentle when that is what is required.

But when unhealthy, the Eight with a Nine wing develops a deep conflict within and becomes unpredictable and dangerous to be around. When they are quiet, you can be sure that there is anger lurking just beneath the surface. This can result in frequent explosions of rage. At their worst, they can descend into a state of paranoid isolation. Intrude and you might be attacked or killed by this antisocial being who lacks compassion or conscience.

The Challenger with a Nine wing will normally not care about what they look like. They would rather just relax. They prefer jobs that mean they will not be overly bothered by other people. A truck driver or a night guard might be a good example. Of course, as with any type, you can find them anywhere!

Advice for The Challenger

1. It is absolutely the case that you value your independence and this is not necessarily a bad thing. However, people need people, whether you like it or not and it is going to be necessary for you to let others in. It is not possible to function in this world as an island and people are not as expendable as you think they are. For example, you might need employees who are loyal and that you can trust. If you alienate them, you will lose them. Similarly, in your personal life, you will be isolated and lonely unless you let people in.

2. Choose your battles wisely! You don't have to win every battle and every argument. Let others have their way from time to time. It is not true power to 'beat' other people all the time. If you feel the need to dominate, it means that your ego is out of control and this will just lead to more unhealthy conflict. Avoid this.

3. Realize your true gifts and capacities, and use your power for good. Restrain yourself if you can foresee that your actions are likely to hurt others. Your real power is to motivate, uplift and to show others what they, too, are capable of. In this way, you can be of great service to others, perhaps helping them in a crisis. This is absolutely the way to inspire loyalty from people.

4. Another quick word about power: those who are attracted to you because of your power and because of this alone, have no real affection for you. They might just be using you as you use them back. Is this really how you want to live your life?

5. People are nicer than you think. So let them in, knowing that this is a sign of true strength and not weakness. When you are mistrustful of others, they will pick up on this and they will not be favorably disposed towards you. Instead, find out who you can trust and show these loyal friends and colleagues your appreciation and devotion.

Enneagram

Enneagram

Chapter Ten - The Peacemaker (Type 9)

A short message from the Author:

Hey! We've made it to the final chapter of the audiobook and I hope you've enjoyed it so far.

If you have not done so yet, I would be incredibly thankful if you could take just a minute to leave a quick review on Audible, even if it's just a sentence or two!

Many readers and listeners don't know how hard reviews are to come by, and how much they help an author.

To do so, just click the 3 dots in the top right corner of your screen inside of your Audible app and hit the "Rate and Review" button.

Then you'll be taken to the "rate and review" page where you can enter your star rating and then write a sentence or two.

It's that simple!

I look forward to reading your review as I personally read every single one.

I am very appreciative as your review truly makes a difference for me. Now back to your scheduled programming.

Fifteen Signs You're a Peacemaker

1. Your dearest wish is to avoid conflict at all costs. This makes some people perceive you as agreeable and others view you as too passive.

2. You are an expert at seeing all points of view and every side of the argument.

3. You have difficulty establishing firm personal boundaries.

Enneagram

4. You are capable of bringing warring parties together and can be instrumental in healing conflicts.

5. You may have a tendency to suffer from lower back pain.

6. You have an active interest in the spiritual side of life.

7. When in an intimate relationship, you have a propensity to give up your agenda in favor of your partner's. You tend to merge with your nearest and dearest. This might result in you neglecting your own personal needs and desires.

8. You dislike having to confront the unpleasant aspects of life. Sometimes you run away from them or live in denial.

9. You are likely an introverted person.

10. Your friends would describe you as easy going, reliable, tolerant and likable.

11. Your inclination is to see the best in other people and to have a trusting and optimistic view of life.

12. You probably find great joy and solace in the natural world.

13. You can sometimes be uncomfortable with change and this can cause you to be conservative – but you are more adaptable than you give yourself credit for!

14. Because you are so modest, some people might make the mistake of taking you for granted or overlooking the often significant contributions that you make.

15. You may have been brought up in an environment where you were taught that conflict is bad and something that should be avoided or denied.

Did anything sound familiar? More than one thing? Then you just might be a Peacemaker.

The Peacemaker Overview

As the name implies, Type Nine on The Enneagram, the Peacemaker, is a seeker of harmony in all areas of life.
Conflict is the enemy itself, as far as the Nine is concerned, and they will avoid it like the plague, if at all feasible. This can be a challenge because, as we all know, conflict is an integral part of life and practically impossible to avoid. So the Peacemaker has to develop strategies to side step these clashes. These often include some manner of withdrawal. This means that Nine is commonly an introvert. Even if the Peacemaker is particularly social, they will find ways to remove themselves from potential strife that may arise within their circle of friends. Because of this, their habit is to go with the flow. Others view them as tolerant and easy going and consequently, easy to like.

The Peacemaker holds a positive view of life and of those that surround them. They are inclined to give people the benefit of the doubt, assuming that they are good sorts until the opposite is proven. They are trusting - as well as trustworthy - and they see the glass as being half-full rather than half-empty. It is common for them to have a stalwart faith - spiritual or otherwise - that things are always working out for them.

A deep-seated desire for the Nine is a sense of connection. They feel this connection with both their fellow humans and with the natural world. The Peacemaker has a genuine connection to nature and will have a sense of being at home wherever it is green. Another arena where the Nine feels at home is parenthood. This type is often an excellent parent - loving and attentive.

Change can sometimes be a challenge for the Type Nine, causing them to feel uneasy and uncomfortable. They do like to stay in their comfort zones! This can translate into quite a conservative attitude towards life. When a Nine is not so well-developed emotionally, they can suffer from a sort of inertia. This can prevent them from taking the action necessary to bring required change into effect. But when change does manifest itself, the Peacemaker may well surprise him or herself with how adaptable they are and how they are, in fact, more than capable of adjusting to their new circumstances. They might also find that they are more resilient than they themselves suspected.

Sometimes they do not give themselves enough credit and this can be quite a problem in their lives. Due to this innate humility and refusal to hog the limelight, the Nine might find him or herself being taken for granted by others. It can almost feel to the Peacemaker like people don't even see them. This lack of validation can be hard to take and they may feel invisible. It is a real shame, as the Peacemaker is capable of and frequently does make significant contributions to many situations. This might show itself as a deep sadness that few are aware of. Or it might be an anger that builds up inside and erupts every so often in a short-lived burst of temper. Or, alternatively, it may reveal itself in passive-aggressive behavior.

It is characteristic of the Nine that they do not always have a definite sense of self and of their own identity. They don't really know who they are! This is only heightened by their penchant to almost merge with their loved ones. They virtually take on the characteristics of those closest to them through a process of identification. So if you are a Nine and you are reading this, it is possible that you do not recognize yourself!

There have been many famous Nines dotted throughout history and prominent in our society today. These include: Queen Elizabeth II, Abraham Lincoln, Carl Jung, Walt Disney, Gloria Steinem, Audrey Hepburn, George Lucas, Princess Grace of Monaco, Claude Monet, Dwight D. Eisenhower, Ronald Reagan, Joseph Campbell, Gary

Cooper, Carlos Santana, Tony Bennett, Sophia Loren, Whoopie Goldberg, Geena Davis, Lisa Kudrow, Woody Harrelson, Kevin Costner, Audrey Hepburn, Annette Bening, Jimmy Stewart, Janet Jackson, Ringo Starr, General Colin Powell, John F. Kennedy Jr., Gerald Forde, Norman Rockwell, Jim Henson and John Goodman.

The Peacemaker Levels

Healthy
Self-Possessed
At their peak, Nines are a joy to be around. And it is a joy, in fact, to be one of them! They feel enormously fulfilled by all that life has given them and they are, therefore, supremely content. They feel totally present within themselves. This causes them to have a sense of, not only independence, but an intense aliveness. They are adept at forming profound relationships with others because of this powerful sense of connection.

Serene
This serenity is often derived from a profound feeling of acceptance. This in turn leads to an enormous sense of stability. They do not doubt themselves and neither do they doubt others. Total trust is the order of the day. There is a perception of ease that they bring to everything that they do, largely because they are patient, good-humored and unselfconscious. They are not trying to be anything that they are not and are genuinely lovely people. There is a simple innocence and a lack of pretense which makes the deeply receptive and healthy Nine a pleasure to be around.

Supportive
The support that the Peacemaker lends to others carries with it a healing and calming influence. They are fantastic at bringing people

together and harmonizing disparate groups. Their optimism reassures others. All the above, together with their often excellent communication skills, can make the Nine a marvellous mediator.

Neutral
Self-Effacing
This mode of conduct is often designed to avoid conflict as much as possible. They do not want to rock the boat so, consequently, will put up with a lot. They might become accommodating to a fault and go along with other people's wishes. This could make them agree to do things that they really do not want to do. This is not a good scenario for anyone involved!

Another way the Five might seek to avoid rocking the boat is by fitting themselves into conventional roles. They do not relish defying other people's expectations. An example of this is a woman becoming a wife and mother. Then, if she returns to work when her children are older, she might go into a traditionally 'feminine' profession such as nursing or hairdressing. This is not the type that commonly challenges stereotypes.

Disengaged
This tendency is due to their wish to avoid problems and conflict of any sort. They might still be taking part in their normal activities but they will be 'checked out' in some way. You might see it in their eyes! They are purposely not paying proper attention. They will not reflect on what is happening because they simply do not want to! They can become complacent, putting up with situations that are not necessarily ideal but are too much trouble to confront. Because of this, they will deny problems and have an impulse to 'sweep them under the rug.' They construct a comforting fantasy world for themselves which is so much more pleasant than reality. The Peacemaker can develop indifference as a coping mechanism, as they refuse to focus on problems and retreat from the real world into self-imposed oblivion.

Resigned

This resignation is in a bid to have peace at any price. A kind of fatalism creeps into the atmosphere. Why bother trying to change anything when it will not work anyway? They can be very stubborn in this stance, causing those around them to get annoyed and frustrated with them as they struggle to get a meaningful response or make things happen. They may indulge in wishful thinking and imagine all sorts of possible magical solutions. They will appease others in order to avoid trouble, even when this is not the healthiest solution.

Unhealthy
Repression

The propensity to hold everything in becomes increasingly unhealthy. It makes the Nine incapable of facing problems as they disassociate themselves from all conflicts. The self cannot be fully actualized in these circumstances and the Peacemaker remains in an undeveloped state. This can actually constitute a danger to those around them as their conduct here can be neglectful.

Disassociation

At this point, the Peacemaker disassociates from life to such an extent that they can barely function. A sort of numbness sets in, while they block out awareness of anything that might upset them.

Catatonic

At this most extreme of lows, the Nine will come across as really disoriented, seemingly becoming nothing more than a shell of their former selves. Psychological conditions can arise, such as schizoid and dependent personality disorders. Multiple personalities are also possible.

The Peacemaker Wings

Type Nine with a One wing (9W1)
The Type Nine with a One wing is a big softy! The influence of the Nine will remain mostly dominant, which will result in the intellectuality of the One filtering in, but not being subject to a great deal of reality-testing. This can cause the Nine with a One wing to develop a set of beliefs that might come across as a bit weird to others. They may be strongly superstitious and 'airy fairy.' The Peacemaker with a One wing can actually make this work for them!
The 9W1 is refined and possesses a manner of elegant poise. In style of dress, they will strive to be as inconspicuous as possible, choosing clothing that will enable them to fit in and become as invisible as possible. Mainstream fashion is the order of the day, with no flamboyant statements being made! They do have a desire to be perfect, however, because of their One wing, so their attire is likely to be neat and tidy.
They are not the workaholics of the Enneagram and can be partial to a pleasant afternoon nap!

When in a healthy state of mind, the One wing lends the type Nine more presence. The light is on *and* someone is home! Concrete results are more likely when the goal-setting One wing exerts its influence. The Peacemaker will become more ambitious but will not be prey to as much perfectionism as the Type One in their pure state. By their efforts, this variant of the Type Nine can affect others in a positive and useful way. However, this is done in a subtle, non-showy manner and the world at large might not be aware of what the Nine has done.
At an advanced psychological level, the Nine with a One wing finds great happiness and fulfilment in the work they do, empowering and teaching other people. They no longer feel the urge to withdraw and involve themselves in a meaningful way in the world. Their dreams

become reality at last and others feel the full benefit of their self-actualized power.

In a not-so-healthy state, the Nine with the One wing will tend to withdraw in a typical Nine way and become more judgmental of the self and others in a typical One way. They might retreat into a comfortable fantasy world and are inevitably disappointed when their real life interactions do not live up to their fantasies.

When bad goes to worse, they become more upset with the discrepancies between their inner fantasy world and outside reality. They cope with this scenario by isolating themselves. Worst case scenario, they might even become psychotic, where they're barely present in a body that gradually goes to rack and ruin.

It would be quite typical for a Peacemaker with a One wing to find work that allows them to use their mind but not necessarily in a very exacting way. Examples might be astrologers, puppeteers and dressmakers.

The Type Nine with an Eight wing (9W8)
These people are the salt of the earth. The Peacemaker with an Eight wing may come across as a little rough-around-the-edges, but cuddly all the same, rather like an over-sized, clumsy puppy, eager for happiness. The inclination is towards gentleness and a lack of sophistication. The Eight will lend the Nine a tad more impulsiveness and forcefulness than they would normally have, but they will back down in the face of too much resistance. The Nine with the Eight wing is not overly eager to rise to every challenge either.

When a Nine with an Eight wing begins to self-actualize, he or she will use their energy and expansiveness to pull themselves out of passivity. They will then become generous, powerful and benevolent. When fully actualized, the Peacemaker is a truly uplifting presence in the world. They are generous, humble and genuinely good. Just being in their sphere of influence is inspiring. They don't do anything, as such. They are just their wonderful selves.

But it's not all rainbows and unicorns! In a state of stress, the Nine with an Eight wing may be paranoid and become almost hermit like in his or her existence. They will be lazy and mistrustful.

At their absolute lowest level, avoidance becomes paramount as the 9W8 spurns all and any human interaction. It is a kind of semi-comatose state and the paranoid persuasions become worse.

In terms of physical appearance, the Nine with an Eight wing is often big and frequently strong. They will seldom be seen in flashy clothing and will strive for normality.

Advice for The Peacemaker

1. Body awareness is very important for the Nine. Exercise will help hugely here. It will allow you to discharge aggression and teach you to concentrate and focus your attention. You will become more aware of your feelings and benefit in terms of self-discipline.

2. Repressed anger causes damage, both to your physical and emotional health. Everybody has negative emotions, including you. When you fail to acknowledge this, you can disturb the harmony you so crave in your relationships. It is far healthier for you to be honest about your feelings - both with yourself and with loved ones - and get issues out in the open, fully aired!

3. You find it deeply difficult to examine pain. But looking honestly at why a relationship has gone wrong, and even worse, admitting to possibly contributing to this problem, is necessary, both for your peace of mind and for ensuring that such a situation does not repeat itself. This is how genuine relationships are created.

4. If it is possible to be *too* nice, then you as a Type Nine are arguably the most likely type on the Enneagram to fall into this trap. Not only is it bad for your own sake to be constantly

acquiescing to other people's needs, especially with loved ones, it is also bad for the other person and for the relationship as a whole. Keeping the peace can sometimes come at a high price. You have to be yourself to have a successful and genuine relationship. Only when you are completely honest about your own needs can you be truly there for the other person.

5. Daydreaming is not a bad past time per se. However, when overused as a means of tuning out of the world around you, this is not so healthy. You should try to engage with people and participate meaningfully in society.

Conclusion

So, we come to the end of this book. Have you read it all? Or have you just skipped to your type or the type you *think* you are? Either way is absolutely fine. This book can be taken as a whole or dipped in and out of, as the reader so desires. The approach you take might depend on your type! A meticulous One may peruse each sentence thoroughly from start to finish, whereas an impulsive Seven, might just skip to the "good bits"! It really doesn't matter, as this book is written for each and every type on the Enneagram.

The aim of this book is to give you a thorough understanding of the Enneagram - the theory behind it, its origins, how it works and how it can work for you. You might be guided by what your friends and loved ones have commented about you and your personality over the years or better still, you may be guided by your own self-knowledge. Best of all, you might be led by your own internal guidance system. Whatever the case, this book has the capacity to add to your self-knowledge and your self-awareness. It is up to you to take it on board and to apply it to your own life. Remember, knowledge is power! Not over others but over the self. Self-mastery is key and knowing yourself is of the utmost importance. Applying this knowledge is gold!

We have covered a lot in the preceding chapters. In the introduction, we learned the origins of the word 'enneagram' and the names of the pioneers in the field, devising the methodology and developing the theory into the Enneagram we know today. Of course, many others who were not named throughout these pages have also made important contributions.

The Enneagram is a complex and useful blend of the wisdom of our predecessors and the insights of modern psychology. As such, it can lend a deep understanding of the self, augmenting what we have already learned throughout our life experiences. It can be used for personal growth, for adding spiritual depth, for working out with whom we are compatible and for understanding our close friends and family members in more depth. We can use it in the area of our careers also. So that is why our boss behaves the way he does! Or why that co-worker can sometimes appear so odd! With insight and understanding comes compassion and hopefully, less conflict too.

This book will help you to understand the positives and negatives of each type, both your own and that of all the people around you. Better understanding all round.

Chapter One taught us about the symbol which represents the Enneagram, how it is constructed out of three separate shapes brought together to make one whole. We have the circle, representing the wholeness of life, the triangle, representing the 'magic' number three and the hexad, an unusual, irregular shape, borrowed from the Sufi tradition, representing the law of seven and the law of octaves.

Within the shape are placed the numbers One to Nine which we now know as the nine Types of the Enneagram and the lines on the symbol demonstrate the connections between the different types.

We have further learned that the Enneagram is not a blunt instrument but an exact tool to be wielded subtly. Accordingly, each person is not made of entirely one personality type. The Enneagram gives you wings! You discover your wing by looking at the numbers on either side of yours and ascertaining for yourself which one most closely aligns with you and your unique character.

We then discovered that the Enneagram and its symbol is structured into three separate triads and that each triad holds a different emotion: One, Eight and Nine are rulers of instinct, Two, Three and Four are in the feeling center, and Five, Six and Seven are in the thinking triad.

You will have noticed how each and every chapter begins with a handy check list, allowing you, the reader, to work out as quickly as possible exactly who you are or to point you in the right direction at least. Think of these check lists as sign posts, pointing you towards your correct destination.

You will have learned that when it comes to the Enneagram, it is more likely to be nature rather than nurture which hold the key. A Type appears to be born rather than made and despite the many and varied changes that happen in our lives, our basic type will remain unchanged, as a constant that can be relied upon. And fundamentally, no type is the 'best' type. We can all strive to be the most wonderful version of ourselves.

Along our journey of discovery about The Enneagram, we also found out about the levels. In other words, that there are three basic levels of development in this system: healthy, average or neutral and unhealthy. Therefore, a healthy One, for example, can look like a totally different creature, and indeed type, than an unhealthy One. Each level is, in turn, divided into the sub-levels, in descending or ascending orders, depending on what way you look at it! Yet another example of the subtlety of the Enneagram. Knowing simply which type you are is not knowing the entire story.

It might be helpful to give you a brief summary of the nine different types and the basic characteristics of each one. So, in numerical order and not in order of importance, I give you the Enneagram:

1. Type One is known as the Reformer or the Perfectionist and, as always, these names reveal a great deal. The Reformer values principles and integrity above all and his or her primary motivation is to be both right and good. They strive for perfection at all times and try to maintain self-control. Quality is of utmost importance and the One will appreciate structure and standards.

The Reformer or Perfectionist has many sterling qualities to offer, such as dignity, discernment, tolerance, serenity and acceptance. Their shadow sides, however, mean that they can be acutely critical of themselves and others, pedantic, uncompromising and judgemental.

2. Type Two is the Helper. Their modus operandi is to be appreciated and liked. They value their relationships above all else and will be generous, kind and self-sacrificing towards this end. They would dearly love to make the world a better place and genuinely try to do this, giving loving attention and support

to those they care about. They shine when it comes to being unconditionally supportive. They are also humble beings, who are capable of practicing healthy self-care. On the not-so-plus side, they might be manipulative and flattering in their mode of giving as they strive to get back what they have given.

3. The Achiever, which is Type Three, wants to be the best! Their priorities include results, efficiency, image and recognition. They are capable of being flexible in order to achieve their goals. Anything for success! At his or her best, The Achiever offers those around them hope and integrity. They are also principled, hard working and receptive. At the worst, they can come across as inconstant and self-important. This is because their sense of self is erroneously based on what they do instead of who they are.

4. Type Four, the Individualist, is driven by his or her intense need to express authenticity and uniqueness. Individualism, as the name suggests, is highly valued, as are self-expression, feelings and purpose. They are romantic souls and beauty will be very important to them, as is meaning. The best of the Four is authenticity and equanimity, sensitivity and contentment. The shadow side of the Individualist shows someone who is melancholic, temperamental and believes themselves to be misunderstood.

5. Type Five, the Investigator, is deeply motivated to know and to understand. They love to make sense of the world around them, valuing knowledge and objectivity. Privacy and independence are priorities for this type and at their best, they are mindful and even visionary. But the darker Five is arrogant, stingy and disconnected from their emotions.

6. Type Six, the Loyalists, are very big on belonging and security and their constant drive is to be safe and well-prepared. As the name implies, they value loyalty and trust and they are responsible sorts. The healthy Six is brave and devoted and possesses a sense of inner knowing. When unhealthy, they can

be doubting, suspicious or anxious and they may fear letting down their defenses and worry to an excessive level.

7. Type Seven, or the Enthusiast wants to experience all and everything that life has to offer, while avoiding pain in the process. They value freedom and they are optimistic and inspired. Life is a big adventure for the Enthusiast with many opportunities along the way to play and be spontaneous. At their best they are serene and content. At their worst, they can be easily distracted, unfocused, impulsive and uncommitted.

8. Type Eight, the Challenger, only likes to act from a place of strength and dislikes displaying their weaknesses. Control is very important to them and they desire to have an impact in their own direct way. They do love a challenge and will protect those that they perceive to be more vulnerable than themselves. At a healthy level, they are caring, strong and approachable. When unhealthy, they can be aggressive and domineering.

9. Type Nine, or the Peacemaker, wants nothing more than to be in harmony with the world. They place great importance on being accommodating and accepting. They love peace and stability while hating conflict. At their best, they are vibrant and self-aware. At their worst, they can be stubborn and inclined to procrastinate.

So I hope that you have found the information provided in this book and the way in which it has been presented to be of use to you. The basics have been covered and expanded upon, and a comprehensive and hopefully engaging guide has been provided. I hope that you have managed to identify your personality type and gain self-knowledge in the process. You should now have all the tools at your disposal.

I wish you the very best of luck on your Enneagram journey and indeed, on your journey throughout life. If there is one thing I would love for you to take away from this book, it is this: that there is no such thing as a good type or a bad type. Each personality type encompasses all aspects and no one type is better than another. As we examine our type and the different levels, my hope for all of us is that we strive for the pinnacle of health and maturity, knowing we are meant for better.

www.ingramcontent.com/pod-product-compliance
Lightning Source LLC
Chambersburg PA
CBHW031107080526
44587CB00011B/862